At Issue

Club Drugs

Other Books in the At Issue Series:

Adaptation and Climate Change

Affirmative Action

Animal Experimentation

Are Teen Curfews Effective?

Can Busy Teens Suceed Academically?

Child Pornography

Do Abstinence Programs Work?

Do Infectious Diseases Pose a Threat?

Do Tax Breaks Benefit the Economy?

Ethanol

The Ethics of Cloning

Fast Food

Is Racism a Serious Problem?

Is Selling Body Parts Ethical?

Nuclear Weapons

Teen Smoking

Teen Suicide

At Issue

Club Drugs

Roman Espejo, Book Editor

GREENHAVEN PRESS
A part of Gale, Cengage Learning

GALE
CENGAGE Learning

Detroit • New York • San Francisco • New Haven, Conn • Waterville, Maine • London

Christine Nasso, *Publisher*
Elizabeth Des Chenes, *Managing Editor*

© 2009 Greenhaven Press, a part of Gale, Cengage Learning.

Gale and Greenhaven Press are registered trademarks used herein under license.

For more information, contact:
Greenhaven Press
27500 Drake Rd.
Farmington Hills, MI 48331-3535
Or you can visit our Internet site at gale.cengage.com

For product information and technology assistance, contact us at

Gale Customer Support, 1-800-877-4253
For permission to use material from this text or product, submit all requests online at
www.cengage.com/permissions

Further permissions questions can be emailed to permissionrequest@cengage.com

Articles in Greenhaven Press anthologies are often edited for length to meet page requirements. In addition, original titles of these works are changed to clearly present the main thesis and to explicitly indicate the author's opinion. Every effort is made to ensure that Greenhaven Press accurately reflects the original intent of the authors. Every effort has been made to trace the owners of copyrighted material.

Cover photograph © Images.com/Corbis.

LIBRARY OF CONGRESS CATALOGING-IN-PUBLICATION DATA

Club drugs / Roman Espejo, book editor.
    p. cm. -- (At issue)
  Includes bibliographical references and index.
  ISBN 978-0-7377-4290-9 (hardcover)
  ISBN 978-0-7377-4289-3 (pbk.)
  1. Ecstasy (Drug). 2. Gamma-hydroxybutyrate. 3. Designer drugs. I. Espejo, Roman, 1977-
  HV5822.M38C586 2009
  362.29'9--dc22
                                                                          2008039334

Printed in the United States of America
1 2 3 4 5 6 7 13 12 11 10 09

Contents

Introduction   **7**

1. The Recreational Use of Club Drugs   **10**
   Is Harmful
   Paul M. Gahlinger

2. GHB and Similar Drugs Can Facilitate Rape   **18**
   Asjylyn Loder

3. Ecstasy Can Be Beneficial in Therapy   **23**
   Brandon Spun

4. Many Drugs Are Not Known as   **30**
   Club Drugs Among Youths
   Denise Rinaldo

5. The Recreational Use of Club Drugs May   **36**
   Increase the Risk of HIV
   Center for AIDS Prevention Studies at the
   University of California, San Francisco (CAPS)

6. The Recreational Use of Ecstasy Is Harmful   **42**
   National Institute on Drug Abuse (NIDA)

7. The Harm of Ecstasy Has Been   **52**
   Misrepresented by Researchers and Reporters
   Ilsa Jerome

8. The Recreational Use of Ecstasy   **58**
   Can Destroy Lives
   Karen de Seve

9. The Psychiatric Use of Ecstasy Can   **62**
   Help Heal Psychological Trauma
   Amy Turner

10. The Illicit Drug Anti-Proliferation Act Deters   **76**
    Selling and Using Club Drugs
    U.S. Drug Enforcement Administration (DEA)

11. The Illicit Drug Anti-Proliferation Act Is Unfair   **81**
    and Threatens Civil Liberties
    Janelle Brown

Organizations to Contact   **88**

Bibliography   **94**

Index   **97**

Introduction

In January 2008, Richard Brunstrom, chief constable of the North Wales Police in Wales, Great Britain, publicly stated that the club drug ecstasy (methylenedioxymethamphetamine or MDMA) is safer than aspirin. He called it "a remarkably safe substance," continuing that there is "a lot of scaremongering and rumor-mongering around ecstasy in particular. It isn't born out by the evidence." An open proponent of drug legalization, Brunstrom stoked outcries for his resignation with his statement from numerous members of his community, the media, and the parents of young people who died from taking ecstasy.

Although Brunstrom's view of ecstasy's safety is extreme, there is a continuum of expert opinion that defends the relative safety of the drug when, for instance, compared to other abused substances. Recently, a group of British researchers led by David Nutt, a member of the Advisory Council on Misuse of Drugs and a psychopharmacologist at Bristol University, evaluated the degree of harm caused by twenty drugs, including ecstasy, cocaine, heroin, and marijuana and legal drugs alcohol and tobacco. In March 2007, the group published their findings: While heroin and cocaine ranked as the most dangerous, alcohol and tobacco placed fifth and ninth respectively, ahead of ecstasy, which placed fourteenth. Why? According to Nutt, an estimated 500,000 Britons take ecstasy every weekend, but only about ten die in ecstasy-related incidents a year. This contrasts with acute alcohol poisoning, which accounts for one fatality in Britain a day, while thousands more die yearly from the long-term effects of alcoholism and smoking. Putting the implications of his group's drug ranking into perspective, Nutt explains, "What we are trying to say is we should review the penalties in the light of the harms and try to have a more proportionate legal response."

In Britain, ecstasy is currently classified as a Class A drug, equivalent to a Schedule I drug in the United States—a substance with a very high potential for abuse and minimal medicinal value that carries the severest legal penalties for distribution and possession.

A much more conservative stance along this continuum of expert opinion proposes that clinically made, pure MDMA can be used safely once or twice in a lifetime as a therapeutic tool under strict supervision—but not as a weekend party pill. Julie Holland, a psychiatry professor at New York University says, "[A] single dose of MDMA—known MDMA—when you're not dancing and overhydrating, but when you're sitting in an office with a psychiatrist, talking about therapeutic material, that is relatively safe." Further distancing herself from the popping of illegally produced ecstasy at clubs, raves, and parties, Holland adds that the "recreational model is unsafe because people don't know what they're taking, they're taking more than they should, and they're taking it more often than they should."

Still, other experts uphold that ecstasy is ultimately harmful—whether the user is raving to synthesized beats in a strobe-lit club or sitting in the controlled environs of a doctor's office. For example, researchers warn that the tendency of MDMA to overheat the body makes it specifically unsafe for clubs or raves. According to Emily Jaehne, doctoral candidate in pharmacology at the University of Adelaide, Australia, "When ecstasy users are taking the drug in nightclubs, they tend to blame the surroundings for their elevated body temperature and just ignore the warning signs. That can be fatal." From her preclinical studies, Jaehn maintains it is dangerously high body temperatures that cause many ecstasy-related deaths in club settings. Furthermore, others contend that the potential of MDMA to cause brain damage deserves consideration during any circumstance or surroundings. According to a 2007 study conducted by a group headed by

Thelma Schilt at University of Amsterdam, Netherlands, small amounts of MDMA lowers the brain's capacity for memory, "Our data indicate that low doses of ecstasy are associated with decreased verbal memory function, which is suggestive for ecstasy-induced neurotoxicity." And in reaction to Nutt's call for a drug reclassification of ecstasy in Great Britain, parliament member David Davis countered, "Thanks to the government's chaotic and confused approach to drugs policy, young people increasingly think it is okay to take drugs. . . . It is vital nothing else leads young people to believe drugs are okay."

The safety of ecstasy use—unlike cocaine, heroin, and methamphetamines—still remains a polarizing topic among researchers, scholars, therapists, policy makers, and, as shown in the North Wales Police case, even law enforcement. In *At Issue: Club Drugs*, authors with expertise in club drugs, and those who have been personally affected by them, offer their viewpoints on this shadowy category of illicit substances.

1

The Recreational Use of Club Drugs Is Harmful

Paul M. Gahlinger

Paul M. Gahlinger is a physician and adjunct professor in the Department of Family and Preventive Medicine at the University of Utah Health Sciences Center, Salt Lake City.

Club drugs are a category of substances that are popular at parties, raves, and nightclubs. The most common of these are MDMA (ecstasy, E, rolls), gamma-hydroxybutyrate (GHB, G, liquid ecstasy), Rohypnol (roofies), and ketamine (Special K, K). These drugs are taken because they are "entactogens"—they are believed to enhance social interaction and create a sense of euphoria. Also, the ease of distribution and use of club drugs as pills, liquids, or powders—along with their relatively low cost and deceiving reputation as being safer drugs than cocaine and heroin—have boosted their popularity. However, each of these club drugs carry real risks that vary from hyperthermia to respiratory depression to seizures and can lead to serious health problems and even death, especially when an overdose occurs or several drugs are ingested at once.

Although alcohol remains the primary "social lubricant," it has been joined by many newer psychoactive drugs that are used to intensify social exeriences. Because of the prevalence of these drugs at dance parties, raves, and nightclubs, they often are referred to as "club drugs." The most prominent club drugs are MDMA (3,4-methylenedioxymethamphetamine), also known as ecstasy; gamma-hydroxybutyrate (GHB); flunitrazepam (Rohypnol); and ketamine (Ketalar)....

Club drugs are favored over other recreational drugs, such as marijuana, lysergic acid diethylamide (LSD), methamphetamine, and opiates, because they are believed to enhance social interaction. They often are described as "entactogens," giving a sense of physical closeness, empathy, and euphoria. MDMA is structurally similar to amphetamine and mescaline, which is a hallucinogen. However, it is not as stimulating or addictive as amphetamine, and is considered much less likely to cause psychosis than LSD and other potent hallucinogens. GHB and Rohypnol are powerful sedative/hypnotic agents. Ketamine is a dissociative anesthetic that produces a dreamy tranquility and disinhibition in small doses. Unlike opiates, these sedatives encourage sociability and seldom cause nausea.

The popularity of these club drugs is due to their low cost and convenient distribution as small pills, powders, or liquids that can be taken orally. Consequently, these drugs are popular among young persons who have been educated about the hazards of drug injection and the dangers of heroin, cocaine, and methamphetamine. However, most users are unaware that MDMA is a type of methamphetamine, and incorrectly assume that substances that appear as pharmaceuticals are safe to use.

Club drugs often are taken together, with alcohol, or with other drugs to enhance their effect. Often, they are misrepresented, adulterated, or entirely substituted for another substance without the users' knowledge. These actions result in an extraordinarily high risk of unanticipated effects and overdose.

In the past 10 years, there has been a generalized decrease in the use of marijuana, cocaine, and heroin in the United States, according to statistics from the Drug Enforcement Administration, the University of Michigan Monitoring the Future Study, the Columbia University National Survey of American Attitudes on Substance Abuse, the Community Epidemiology Working Group, and the Partnership for a Drug-Free America. However, during this same period, the use of club drugs has dramatically increased. A 2001–2002 Chicago household survey of 18- to 40-year-old persons showed that 38 percent had attended a rave, and 49 percent of these had a taken a club drug. One Australian study showed that only 8 percent of club-goers had not consumed any psychoactive substance.

MDMA

MDMA was developed in 1914 as an appetite suppressant, but animal tests were unimpressive, and it was never tested in humans. In 1965, psychiatrists prescribed the drug to break through psychologic defenses as an "empathy agent." By 1985, illegal laboratories were producing the drug for recreational use, and it was classified as a schedule I controlled substance.

MDMA has become the most common stimulant found in dance clubs and is available at 70 percent of raves. MDMA usually is sold as small tablets of variable colors imprinted with popular icons or words. A high proportion of MDMA pills are adulterated with substances such as caffeine, dextromethorphan, pseudoephedrine, or potent hallucinogens such as LSD, paramethoxyamphetamine (PMA), methylenedioxyamphetamine (MDA), N-ethyl-3, 4-methylenedioxyamphetamine (MDEA), and 4-bromo-2,5-dimethoxyamphetamine (2-CB). Many of these substances are "designer drugs" that are illicitly manufactured variants of pharmaceuticals and have intentional and unintentional effects. For example, MDEA ("Eve"), 2-CB, and PMA ("death") are substituted amphetamines but have primarily hallucinogenic, and often unpleasant, effects.

MDMA ingestion increases the release of serotonin, dopamine, and norepinephrine from presynaptic neurons and prevents their metabolism by inhibiting monoamine oxidase. Effects of an oral dose appear within 30 to 60 minutes and last up to eight hours. A quicker onset of action can be achieved by snorting the powder of a crushed tablet. Users of MDMA describe initial feelings of agitation, a distorted sense of time, and diminished hunger and thirst, followed by euphoria with a sense of profound insight, intimacy, and well-being. To further enhance the sensory effects, users often wear fluorescent necklaces, bracelets, and other accessories, and apply mentholated ointment on their lips or spray menthol inhalant on a surgical mask. Unpleasant side effects of MDMA include trismus [jaw clenching] and bruxism [tooth grinding], which can be reduced by sucking on a pacifier or lollipop.

Adverse effects of MDMA ingestion result from sympathetic overload and include tachycardia, mydriasis, diaphoresis, tremor, hypertension, arrhythmias, parkinsonism, esophoria (tendency for eyes to turn inward), and urinary retention. However, the most troublesome potential outcome of MDMA ingestion is hyperthermia and the associated "serotonin syndrome." Serotonin syndrome is manifested by grossly elevated core body temperature, rigidity, myoclonus, and autonomic instability; it results in end-organ damage, rhabdomyolysis and acute renal failure, hepatic failure, adult respiratory distress syndrome, and coagulopathy.

MDMA ingestion directly causes a rise in antidiuretic hormone. Heat from the exertion of dancing in a crowded room coupled with the MDMA-induced hyperthermia can lead easily to excessive water intake and severe hyponatremia. Neurologic effects include confusion, delirium, paranoia, headache, anorexia, depression, insomnia, irritability, and nystagmus, all of which may continue for several weeks.

Two days after ingestion of MDMA, users typically experience depression consistent with serotonin depletion, which may be severe. One study showed that, compared with alcohol withdrawal, persons who are withdrawing from MDMA were more depressed, irritable, and unsociable. Repeated use of MDMA has been associated with cognitive deficits in animals and humans, with potentially permanent memory impairment.

Chronic use of GHB may produce dependence and a withdrawal syndrome that includes anxiety, insomnia, tremor, and in severe cases, treatment-resistant psychoses.

A number of products are sold legally as "herbal ecstasy." These products, available in health food stores or on the Internet, contain stimulants such as ephedra, caffeine, and guarana, with variable additions of common herbs or vitamins. Users of these products may believe they are safe alternatives to MDMA, but several cases of toxic overdose have been reported from the intense stimulation of ephedrine or excessive caffeine.

GHB

GHB is a derivative of the inhibitory neurotransmitter g-aminobutyric acid and occurs naturally in the central nervous system, where it is believed to mediate sleep cycles, body temperature, cerebral glucose metabolism, and memory.

GHB was first synthesized in France in 1960 as an anesthetic. It later achieved popularity as a recreational drug and a nutritional supplement marketed to bodybuilders. Nonprescription sales in the United States were banned in 1990 because of adverse effects, including uncontrolled movements and depression of the respiratory and central nervous systems (CNS). In 2000, with 60 deaths reported from overdose and concern over its use as a "date rape" drug, GHB was reclassified as a schedule I controlled substance. In 2002, sodium oxybate, a formulation of GHB, was approved for the treatment of narcolepsy and classified as schedule III. Recently, sodium oxybate has been studied as a treatment for alcohol withdrawal.

GHB is easily manufactured from industrial chemicals. Internet Web sites offer instructions for home production and sell kits with the requisite materials. GHB is chemically related to gamma butyrolactone and 1,4-butanediol, which are metabolized in the body to GHB.

The salty powder usually is dissolved in water and sold at $5 to $10 per dose. Overdose is common because the strength of the solution is often unknown. The unpleasant salty or soapy taste may be masked in flavored or alcoholic beverages. Effects of GHB appear within 15 to 30 minutes of oral ingestion and peak at 20 to 60 minutes, depending on whether it is mixed with food. Toxicity is increased if taken with alcohol or other CNS depressants.

GHB produces euphoria, progressing with higher doses to dizziness, hypersalivation, hypotonia, and amnesia. Overdose may result in Cheyne-Stokes respiration, seizures, coma, and death. Coma may be interrupted by agitation, with flailing activity described similar to a drowning swimmer fighting for air. Bradycardia and hypothermia are reported in about one third of patients admitted to a hospital for using GHB and appear to be correlated with the level of consciousness. Chronic use of GHB may produce dependence and a withdrawal syndrome that includes anxiety, insomnia, tremor, and in severe cases, treatment-resistant psychoses.

Rohypnol

Flunitrazepam, marketed as Rohypnol, is a potent benzodiazepine with a rapid onset. Manufactured by Roche Laboratories, it is available in more than 60 countries in Europe and Latin America for preoperative anesthesia, sedation, and treatment of insomnia. In the United States, imported Rohypnol came to prominence in the 1990s as an inexpensive recreational sedative and a "date rape" drug. The tablets are sold on the street for $0.50 to $5 a piece.

In a single 1- or 2-mg dose, Rohypnol reduces anxiety, inhibition, and muscular tension with a potency that is approximately 10 times that of diazepam (Valium). Higher doses produce anterograde amnesia, lack of muscular control, and loss of consciousness. Effects occur about 30 minutes after ingestion, peak at two hours, and may last up to eight to 12 hours. The effects are much greater with the concurrent ingestion of alcohol or other sedating drugs. Some users experience hypotension, dizziness, confusion, visual disturbances, urinary retention, or aggressive behavior.

Like other benzodiazepines, chronic use of Rohypnol can produce dependence. The withdrawal syndrome includes headache, tension, anxiety, restlessness, muscle pain, photosensitivity, numbness and tingling of the extremities, and increased seizure potential.

Ketamine

Ketamine was derived from phencyclidine (PCP) in the 1960s for use as a dissociative anesthetic. It causes anesthesia without respiratory depression by inhibiting the neuronal uptake of norepinehrine, dopamine, serotonin, and glutamate activation in the *N*-methyl-*D*-aspartate receptor channel. This agent can cause bizarre ideations and hallucinations—side effects that limited its medical use but appealed to recreational drug users.

Ketamine is difficult to manufacture; therefore, most of the illicit supply is diverted from human and veterinary anesthesia products. As a pharmaceutical, ketamine is distributed in a liquid form that can be ingested or injected. In clubs, it usually has been dried to a powder and is smoked in a mixture of marijuana or tobacco, or is taken intranasally. A typical method uses a nasal inhaler, called a "bullet" or "bumper";

an inhalation is called a "bump." Ketamine often is taken in "trail mixes" of methamphetamine, cocaine, sildenafil citrate (Viagra), or heroin.

Effects of ketamine ingestion appear rapidly and last about 30 to 45 minutes, with sensations of floating outside the body, visual hallucinations, and a dream-like state. Along with these "desired" effects, users also commonly experience confusion, anterograde amnesia, and delirium. They also may experience tachycardia, palpitations, hypertension, and respiratory depression with apnea. "Flashbacks" or visual disturbances can be experienced days or weeks after ingestion. Some chronic users become addicted and exhibit severe withdrawal symptoms that require detoxification.

Because club drugs are illicitly obtained and often are adulterated or substituted, they must be considered as unknown substances. . . . Web sites can be helpful in identifying the rapidly changing appearances of these substances.

2

GHB and Similar Drugs Can Facilitate Rape

Asjylyn Loder

Asjylyn Loder is a New York City–based writer.

GHB (gamma-hydroxybutyrate) and its chemical cousins, or analogs, are known among partygoers for their euphoric properties. However, its other properties—which includes dizziness, incapacitation, and blackouts—have earned the substance its reputation as a date-rape drug. In fact, sexual predators favor GHB because a small dose slipped in a beverage can cripple a victim for hours within ten minutes, leaving her or him with little to no recollection of being assailed. Because of its high potential for overdose, numerous victims poisoned with GHB by sexual predators at clubs, bars, and parties have died or have been hospitalized. Yet, despite a federal crackdown and toughened date-rape drug laws, GHB and its analogs are still available for sale on the Internet.

Years after the fatal poisoning of Michigan teen Samantha Reid by a so-called date-rape drug, these types of narcotics remain widely available in the United States despite crackdowns.

[On January 16, 2004], a Missouri judge will sentence two dealers of a rape drug to up to 30 years in prison. The mother-and-son team Cassandra and Joshua Harvey pled guilty to selling 10 million doses to online customers of 1,4-butanediol,

Asjylyn Loder, "U.S. Drugs: Date Rape Drugs Still Available, Despite Crackdown," *Women's E-News*, January 2004. Reproduced by permission. www.womensenews.org.

or BD, one of several similar date-rape drugs that cause swift and disabling intoxication that leaves victims with little memory of events.

The drugs that the Harveys were caught dealing converts to GHB (gamma hydroxy butyrate) in the body. Their sentencing comes five years to the day after the fatal poisoning of Rockwood, Mich., teen Samantha Reid, who died on Jan. 17, 1999 after three male teens dosed her soda with GHB at a Detroit-area party.

"Samantha was in the hospital on life support, and I asked the emergency-room physician what put my daughter in this state," Judith Clark, Reid's mother told *Women's eNews*. It was the first time Clark heard of GHB, marketed as a nutritional supplement and sleep-aid.

Reid, then 15, died the next day.

Three years earlier, Hillory Farias, a Texas teen, died after unknowingly drinking a GHB-laced soft drink.

GHB use in sexual assaults has surpassed the widely known date-rape drug Rohypnol. . . .

Following her daughter's death, Clark lobbied the then president, Bill Clinton, to sign the Hillory J. Farias and Samantha Reid Date Rape Drug Prohibition Act of 2000, classifying GHB as an illegal Schedule 1 drug like heroin.

Drugs Still Easy to Find

Despite the stricter laws, GHB and its chemical cousins, called analogs, remain cheap and readily available.

Efforts by *Women's eNews* to purchase analogs led to several products on dozens of Web sites. One 4-ounce bottle of a liquid sleep-aid from Avant Labs called Tranquili-G, sells for $45.97 and purports to contain "4-pentanolide (patent pending)," a pseudonym for a GHB analog. Caleb Stone, president and chief executive officer of Oklahoma City–based Avant

Labs, said he discontinued production nine months ago, although dozens of Web sites appear to still be marketing the product.

On the street, a single dose of GHB costs between $5 to $25 and is popular among club goers for its euphoric effects and among bodybuilders, who believe it stimulates growth hormones. The drug is also widely viewed as the drug of choice for sexual assailants who know that small amounts can disable a victim within 10 minutes.

"GHB is one of the drugs most often used to commit drug-facilitated sexual assault," said Ronald Strong, supervisor of the national drug threat assessment unit at the U.S. National Drug Intelligence Center in Johnstown, Penn., a division of the Department of Justice. GHB use in sexual assaults has surpassed the widely-known date-rape drug Rohypnol, known as roofies, he said.

There are no statistics on how many drug-facilitated sexual assaults take place each year. The Drug Abuse Warning Network, a surveillance program run by the U.S. Department of Health and Human Services, counted 3,330 emergency-department mentions of GHB in 2002. That's up from 58 in 1994, but down from a peak of 4,989 in 2000.

In March 2002, a Sioux Falls, S.D., woman reported to police that her husband used a sleep-aid containing an analog of GHB to sexually assault both her and their teen-age babysitter, according to a 2002 Drug Enforcement Administration report.

GHB analogs are common industrial solvents. A 2002 FBI report estimated the industrial consumption of the GHB analog BD, at 387,000 metric tons in 2001.

Cassandra Harvey bought 55-gallon drums of BD by claiming to manufacture a type of cleanser. The Harveys had more than 2,000 gallons of BD when they were arrested, according to the Missouri U.S. Attorney's office.

They were arrested in September 2002, as part of the Drug Enforcement Administration's "Operation Webslinger" crackdown on online GHB dealers, which led to the arrest of 35 people, closure of three labs and seizure of more than 25 million doses.

"Since then, the distribution of GHB and GHB analogs on the Internet appears to have decreased," said Paula Berezansky, an intelligence analyst with the National Drug Intelligence Center. "However, the drugs are still available over the Internet."

Barriers to Prosecuting

Drug-facilitated sexual assaults involving GHB remain notoriously hard to prosecute. "One of our problems is that the system fails these victims even when we get these victims in time," said Trinka Porrata, a retired Los Angeles police officer and a nationally recognized expert on so-called club drugs, that is substances used to heighten sexual experiences and often for date rape.

"The first barrier is that many in law enforcement don't have any training on it," said Porrata. "Because her story does not make any sense, they think, 'This broad's crazy. She's drunk.'" Training police officers to distinguish between GHB and alcohol is crucial, Porrata said, but "not a high priority for law enforcement."

The drugs leave the body between 8 hours and 24 hours and a victim may be incapacitated for much of that time. She might wake up in a strange place or without her clothes, with little recollection of events.

There is no standard rape kit nationwide, but rape kits rarely contain a urine collection cup. Emergency room personnel may not be trained to take urine samples immediately if a sexual-assault victim shows signs of having been drugged. Porrata has seen evidence lost because a victim was allowed to use the bathroom while she waited for the doctor.

Critical lapses in evidence collection are often compounded by confusion as to how the drugs work. Witnesses, judges and juries may not realize that the victim's drunken-like behavior resulted from being drugged. District attorneys may not have the budget for an expert witness to explain GHB to a jury, Porrata said.

The three teens involved in spiking Reid's drink are serving up to 15 years in prison for involuntary manslaughter. The host of the party where the poisoning took place received five years as an accessory to manslaughter and will be released on March 24, 2004.

At their sentencing hearing in 2000, Clark told the judge, "Your honor, the nation is watching today," and asked the judge to set an example by sentencing the men to the maximum penalty.

[In March 2003], a Michigan appeals court threw out the sentences on a technicality, arguing that the prosecution contradicted itself by claiming that the manslaughter was involuntary but the poisoning intentional. If the Michigan Supreme Court upholds the ruling, all four men will be eligible for immediate release. [The ruling was overturned.]

3

Ecstasy Can Be Beneficial in Therapy

Brandon Spun

Brandon Spun is a reporter for Insight on the News.

MDMA, which is the chemical in the illegal club drug ecstasy, may be beneficial when used as part of treatment for depression. Before it was banned, ecstasy was used in therapy for some patients and showed promise, with no deaths being reported. Its advocates claim that the reason the drug was banned was because of its abuse at clubs, which is the reason the drug has such a negative image. While scientists do not know much about ecstasy's long-term effects on the brain, some fear that ecstasy causes brain damage. If approved for therapeutic use, ecstasy would be used in a controlled way and would be part of a broader treatment for depression, unlike another drug used to treat depression, Prozac, which also has serious potential side effects.

The first U.S.-approved tests on the therapeutic effects of MDMA, the active chemical in the "nightclub drug" known as ecstasy, may begin in a few months, 17 years after it was made illegal and 90 years after it was invented. At issue is whether this powerful neurotoxin can be an effective tool for therapy. What is certain is that scientists know as much about MDMA's long-term effects on the brain as they do about most commonly prescribed psychotropics—that is, very little.

A recent Fox News special on the lasting effects of ecstasy had a psychiatrist from Emory University in Atlanta displaying before-and-after slides of an ecstasy user's brain. He claimed the slides demonstrated lasting damage. But when questioned by INSIGHT, the expert knew neither whose research he had presented nor details of the alleged tests. Misinformation and mythology, critics say, are as common in the war on drugs as in the mental-health community.

Is Prozac Really Beneficial?

Many drugs have unintended side effects, but while TV commercials quietly tag on messages that say a pill might cause heart problems or that pregnant women should not handle them, these warnings pale in comparison to the potential dangers of mood-altering drugs. Here are a few side effects of one psychotropic: paralysis, coma, hysteria, suicidal [ideation] and violent behaviors, arrhythmia, gastrointestinal hemorrhage, ulcers, colitis, hepatitis, incontinence, gout, goiter, hyperthyroidism, eczema, psoriasis, osteoporosis, abortion, glaucoma, deafness, taste loss and sexual dysfunction.

That drug is Prozac, the most widely prescribed pharmaceutical in the country. And though its mood-altering chemical compound has been used by millions, little is reported about its potentially deadly side effects. Its manufacturers get by with claims that the effects listed above are rare, occurring in less than one in 1,000 users. But, as INSIGHT has reported, psychotropics often have been linked with cases in which people have been involved in bizarre and deadly incidents.

Prozac, as well as Paxil and Zoloft, are serotonin selective reuptake inhibitors (SSRIs) that increasingly have been prescribed for depression. Serotonin, a neurotransmitter, is a chemical that facilitates communication within the brain. It is contended that serotonin allows one to experience happiness when it is released into the synapses, the empty spaces between nerve cells. Antidepressants are supposed to prevent the reabsorption of serotonin so that the "happiness experience" can last longer.

If so, people for whom SSRIs are prescribed should have lower levels of serotonin than happy people. But there is little evidence of this. "The categories of mental illness are so porous as to allow everyday unhappiness to pass into the category of a more significant disease," says Ronald Dworkin, a physician at the Hudson Institute in Indianapolis. The way these psychotropics affect the emotions is more mysterious, and more threatening, than practitioners who use them have dared to admit.

Some patients [using ecstasy] reported overnight breakthroughs and couples treated together solved long-term issues.

It nonetheless has become increasingly common to prescribe these drugs to people suffering from milder forms of depression. As Kelly Patricia O'Meara reported in INSIGHT, "six million children in the United States between the ages of 6 and 18 are taking mind-altering drugs."

Dworkin and others argue against use of psychotropics altogether. But some suggest the point is not that Prozac and other psychotropics never are beneficial, but that often they are administered as take-home solutions rather than in conjunction with therapy and careful observation. And, even when SSRIs are being used in therapy, they may be doing more than "freeing" the mind. No one knows what damage may be done to the brain by a lifetime of psychotropic treatment.

Hope for Ecstasy

But now some doctors are hoping to use ecstasy on their patients.

This may not be as strange as it seems. Before the drug was banned in the mid-1980s, doctors claimed to have been using it in therapy with success. Some patients reported overnight breakthroughs and couples treated together solved long-term issues. Its advocates claim the reason the drug was made illegal, and remains so, is its rampant abuse at nightclubs.

In some ways MDMA is very different from SSRIs. Instead of just affecting serotonin, it floods neurons with several neurotransmitters, including dopamine and noradrenaline. And, unlike Prozac, MDMA appears to reduce depression, anxiety and other emotional ailments immediately.

Rick Doblin is the president of the Multidisciplinary Association for Psychedelic Studies (MAPS), an organization dedicated to MDMA research. On Nov. 2, 2001, MAPS was the first group to receive Food and Drug Administration approval for therapeutic MDMA research. Doblin hopes this research will begin in a few months, after he receives approval from the University of South Carolina's Institutional Review Board. He discussed some of the misconceptions about the drug with INSIGHT.

MDMA would be used under strict control and in small doses during limited therapy sessions over a lifetime.

Doblin estimates that for roughly every 2 million users of ecstasy there is one directly related death. And, as a designer drug, ecstasy often is cut with sometimes-deadly substances that he thinks are responsible for a majority of related deaths. Though, contrary to the urban myth, he says, heroin is rarely if ever used to cut the drug. And Doblin believes concern about ecstasy deaths should not deter approval of research. The most common MDMA-related deaths, he says, are from overheating or overhydration. "In the temperature-controlled environment of therapy, where a patient will be drinking a regimented quantity of water, one does not run that risk," Doblin claims.

No one ever has died in MDMA therapy, and scattered research abroad suggests it may prove helpful in relieving certain acute stress. Doblin specifically cites MDMA research on [R]ape victims in Spain that has not yet been published. The U.S. research would focus on male and female victims of criminal and sexual abuse. An Israeli study will focus on victims of war and terrorism. Eventually Doblin hopes to test MDMA as a direct competitor against psychotropics. "So this may be why companies haven't jumped on the bandwagon," he says.

The Case Against Ecstasy

Doblin knows there are a few other reasons, too. For one, selling MDMA is not a marketer's dream. Not only does it have a bad image, but the patent has run out, so no company would have an opportunity for the enormous profits of, say, Prozac or Zoloft.

Also, as noted, MDMA is not meant as a take-home drug. While most SSRIs are taken daily by users, MDMA would be used under strict control and in small doses during limited therapy sessions over a lifetime. So MDMA lacks both the potential for harm and the enormous profitability of the standard psychotropic—unless, of course, it is abused as a street drug.

Doblin admits that he does worry about the widespread medicating of society with psychotropics and other drugs. "It is a double-edged sword," he says. He rejects unauthorized medication. In uncontrolled settings, MDMA is famous for having triggered anxiety attacks and psychotic breakdowns. People on ecstasy have experienced severe depressive periods that have sent some to hospitals begging for tranquilizers. The drug's proponents are aware of this. They respond that, under proper controls, MDMA frees people to experience emotions and memories they otherwise were unable to confront—and that without therapy they are left to face them on their own. "A person in therapy is prepared to do serious introspection. Someone else may not be," Doblin says.

Possible Brain Damage

The trouble is that studies conducted by neurologist George Ricaurte of the Johns Hopkins School of Medicine associate serotonin depletion and brain damage with use of MDMA. Ricaurte studied ecstasy users from the standard population (who also may have used other drugs). Their serotonin levels were compared with those of drug-free students, as though they should have been the same. Serotonin levels were lower amongst drug users. But in a Swiss study, the opposite results were found when testing individuals before and after ecstasy use, although studies have disagreed on what counts as "use" and "abuse."

But the most serious concern is that MDMA may cause brain damage—may, in fact, be a neurotoxin.

When the brain is damaged, neural pathways often become misshapen. In a study on monkeys performed by Ricaurte this did not occur, but the neural pathways bundled up and reorganized, suggesting changes. Those changes were interpreted as damage by some, though unlike Prozac or Ritalin, high levels of MDMA have not been found to cause starlike lesions in neural pathways. James O'Callaghan, a neurotoxicologist at the Centers for Disease Control and Prevention, has addressed this inconsistency in the pharmacological community, calling it a "double standard."

While long-term effects of psychotropics are dubious, less tenuous are the links between these drugs and horrific psychotic episodes, sometimes associated with high-profile killings. Experts readily admit their ignorance concerning lasting impact of psychotropics on the brain, but they downplay or ignore what is known about their immediate and troubling effects.

4

Many Drugs Are Not Known as Club Drugs Among Youths

Denise Rinaldo

Denise Rinaldo is a journalist who covers teen issues.

The term club drugs emerged a decade ago to describe the drugs youths used at raves, all-night dance parties, and nightclubs. These include ecstasy, ketamine, GHB, rohypnol, and methamphetamines. The new generation of adolescents, however, does not call them club drugs. In fact, the majority of experimentation and use of these drugs now happens at parties, with friends at home, and—in the near-tragic ecstasy case of "Ariel"—even at school-related events. But lack of awareness of the risks of club drugs does not mean youths will not use them. Rather, it highlights today's youths' susceptibility to the dangers of ecstasy, ketamine, GHB, and other illicit substances, which are deceptively marketed under various names and in candy colors as harmless fun.

"I thought I was going to die," says Ariel Trevino, remembering the terrifying day [in 2006] when she had her first experience with a drug known to scientists as MDMA or 3,4 methylenedioxymethamphetamine.

Ariel, 14, was with friends watching a football game at her high school in Merced, California, when she tried the drug. "I was told it only gets you a little bit high," she says.

The drug was in pill form and the pills were colorful. To Ariel, they looked like candy. She swallowed one and a half of them. For the next half an hour, she didn't feel much of anything. Then, things went horribly wrong.

Signs of Trouble

"I was numb from the waist down," Ariel says. "I couldn't walk, so my friend was helping me get to the bleachers. Then, I remember somebody throwing me over his shoulders and running me down to the field. I was shaking. Then, I guess I passed out."

MDMA, the drug that Ariel took, has a nonscientific name too: Ecstasy. It goes by other names as well. Some people call it E. Kids at Ariel's school call it Thizz.

Ecstasy is one of a group of drugs that have been called club drugs. The drugs ketamine, GHB, rohypnol, and methamphetamine are also part of the group. The term club drugs originated about 10 years ago when abuse of the drugs was increasing. This was because teens and young adults were using them at nightclubs and at all-night parties called raves.

Still Dangerous

Today, fewer teens are abusing club drugs, which is good news. The bad news is that too many teens still fall prey to the drugs. Also, there is evidence that fewer teens understand the dangers of club drugs. A study done last year by the National Institute on Drug Abuse found a significant drop in the percentage of young people who believe that Ecstasy is dangerous.

Today, most teens who abuse Ecstasy, methamphetamine, ketamine, GHB, or rohypnol don't call them club drugs. Ariel had never heard the term before she talked to *Choices*. "I've never heard of kids referring to them as club drugs," says Bessie Oster, a program director at Phoenix House, a nationwide substance-abuse service organization. That's probably because club drug abuse is now less likely to happen in clubs or at raves.

These days, experts say, teens who abuse the drugs do so in many places—at parties, at home with friends, or even, as in Ariel's case, at sports events. Sometimes, the drugs' names are changed. Occasionally, the drugs contain impurities like other drugs and chemicals that make them even more dangerous than usual.

Emergency

This brings us back to Ariel. After passing out on the football field, Ariel was rushed to a hospital by ambulance. She woke up there with "a tube up my nose and down my throat so I could breathe, and all kinds of wires all over my body," she says. Her mother, brother, and stepfather showed up in a panic. "I remember seeing them crying," Ariel says. She was so confused that she kept calling for her father, who had died the year before.

Doctors at the hospital tested Ariel's blood. It turned out that the pills she took contained Ecstasy, methamphetamine, and other impurities. "I'm really lucky that my life was spared," Ariel says. "That was my first time taking Ecstasy, and it's going to be my last."

To find out more about club drugs and their dangers, read [below]. Some of the drugs listed are made in illegal laboratories. . . .

MDMA. What It Is: Acts as a stimulant and hallucinogen. MDMA causes feelings of high energy and warmth. Also causes nausea, sweating, teeth-clenching, muscle cramps, and blurred vision.

Street Names: Ecstasy, Adam, Bean, E, Essence, Hug, Lover's Speed, Stacy, Thizz, X, XTC

How It's Taken: Usually in pill form. Pills are often pastel-colored and stamped with designs. It is also sold in liquid and caplet form.

Immediate Dangers: Ecstasy takes a long time to break down after it enters the body. As a result, taking a lot of Ecstasy increases the risk of overdosing. An overdose or adverse reaction can cause the body temperature to skyrocket. This can cause the kidneys, liver, and heart to fail, which results in death. Other risks include increased blood pressure, hallucinations, and seizures.

Long-Term Dangers: Addiction, depression, severe anxiety, loss of ability to recall information.

Hidden Risk: Ecstasy often contains other drugs such as methamphetamine or cocaine that can interact dangerously with each other or cause harm on their own.

GHB. What It Is: A central nervous system depressant that causes feelings of both calmness and euphoria. Can also cause drowsiness, nausea, and vomiting.

Street Names: G, Liquid Ecstasy, Liquid E, GBH, Grievous Bodily Harm, Scoop, Soap

How It's Taken: Taken by mouth, GHB is available as a clear, odorless liquid or as a white powder.

Immediate Dangers: Unconsciousness, seizures, and severely slow breathing, all of which can lead to death.

Long-Term Dangers: Brain and other organ damage caused by lack of oxygen during seizures or by severely slow breathing.

Hidden Risks: Combining alcohol and GHB increases the depressant effect of both. The combination can be fatal. Also, because it is clear and odorless, GHB is used as a predatory drug. Victims become drowsy and confused, and thus vulnerable to rape, assault, and robbery.

Methamphetamine. What It Is: An extremely addictive stimulant that is made using poisonous materials, such as battery acid. Creates feelings of confusion and paranoia. Makes a person more active, but decreases appetite.

Street Names: Black Beauties, Chalk, Crystal Meth, Glass, Go-Fat, Ice, Meth, Poor Man's Cocaine, Tina

How It's Taken: As pills, powder, or crystal. It is swallowed, smoked, snorted, or injected.

Immediate Dangers: Rapid or irregular heartbeat, dangerously high body temperature, high blood pressure, convulsions, psychosis.

Long-Term Dangers: Addiction, skin ulcers, severe dental problems, short-term memory damage, brain damage.

Hidden Risk: Methamphetamine labs harm the environment. The chemicals released when the drug is made pollute water sources and soil.

Rohypnol. What It Is: A central nervous system depressant that is sold in Europe as a sleep aid but is illegal in the United States. Causes feelings of drowsiness, calmness, and euphoria.

Street Names: Circles, The Date Rape Drug, Rib, Roachies, Roofies, Roche (pronounced ro-SHAY)

How It's Taken: In pill form. The pills are swallowed or dissolved in liquid.

Immediate Dangers: Loss of muscle control, unconsciousness, blackouts, and amnesia.

Long-Term Dangers: Addiction. Withdrawal symptoms include extreme anxiety, muscle pain, hallucination, and seizures, which can lead to heart failure and death.

Hidden Risks: Taking alcohol with rohypnol increases the sedative effect of both. The combination can be fatal. Rohypnol is also used as a predatory drug.

Ketamine. What It Is: A tranquilizer and central nervous system depressant that causes hallucinations, dreamlike states, delirium, and amnesia.

Street Names: Cat Valium, Breakfast Cereal, K, Jet, Special K, Super Acid

How It's Taken: Available as a liquid, a pill, or a powder. It is taken by mouth, injected, or smoked.

Immediate Dangers: Muscle spasms or paralysis; extremely slow breathing that can lead to death; feelings of disconnection and inability to feel pain.

Long-Term Dangers: Addiction, paranoia, flashbacks.

Hidden Risks: Because ketamine causes feelings of disconnectedness, users often make bad decision—such as walking into traffic or having unsafe sex. Ketamine is also used as a predatory drug.

5

The Recreational Use of Club Drugs May Increase the Risk of HIV

Center for AIDS Prevention Studies at the University of California, San Francisco (CAPS)

The Center for AIDS Prevention Studies at the University of California, San Francisco, is an organization that conducts domestic and international research, aiming to prevent the acquisition of HIV and to optimize health outcomes among HIV-infected individuals.

The use of club drugs such as MDMA (ecstasy), ketamine (Special K), and gamma-hydroxybutyrate (GHB) may heighten an individual's risks of being infected with HIV. Several factors contribute to this risk: club drugs lower inhibitions, enhance sexual endurance, and impair judgment. This increases the likelihood of engaging in unsafe sexual practices, including unprotected sex, sex with multiple partners, and sex with persons of unknown HIV status. In a survey of gay men who attend "circuit parties" (large gay dance parties that last for days), a high percentage reports using MDMA, GHB, and ketamine. Similarly, a survey of individuals who attend raves also reveals that the use of such drugs at these events may be high. Therefore, it is highly recommended that these communities confront the link between club drugs and unsafe sex and the pressures to engage in both.

Center for AIDS Prevention Studies at the University of California, San Francisco (CAPS), "How Do Club Drugs Impact HIV Prevention?" CAPS.UCSF.Edu, July 2004. Reproduced by permission.

Club drugs are illegal drugs that are often, although not exclusively, used at dance clubs, raves and circuit parties. Drugs often referred to as club drugs include: MDMA (ecstasy), methamphetamine (crystal meth, speed), GHB (liquid X), Ketamine (special K) and, less often, Viagra and amyl nitrites (poppers). These drugs also are often used outside of clubs and parties.

Raves are large parties featuring house or techno music and visual effects. Mostly younger people attend raves. Circuit parties are a series of large, predominantly gay parties lasting several days and nights in a row that are frequented mostly by younger and older middle-class white men. They occur annually in different cities.

Some of the physical and psychological effects of club drugs include: elevated mood, increased empathy, altered vision, sensations and emotions, increased alertness, decreased appetite, relaxation, increased physical energy and/or self-confidence. Many people use drugs recreationally with few or no immediate repercussions. Misuse of club drugs can lead to problems with toxicity (from the drugs themselves or from interactions with other drugs), with legal issues and sometimes with addiction. Persons using one or more club drugs during sex often report engaging in extremely high HIV-risk behaviors.

Club drugs can cause a variety of non-HIV-related health risks. This fact sheet will focus on sexual and drug-using HIV-risk behaviors that can occur with club drug use.

Who Uses Club Drugs?

Most of the research on club drugs has been with gay men, mainly because HIV prevalence and risk of infection are high among gay men. Use of club drugs varies by different populations and by geography.

A survey of gay male circuit party attenders in San Francisco found that 80% used ecstasy, 66% ketamine, 43% methamphetamines, 29% GHB, 14% Viagra and 12% poppers during their most recent out-of-town weekend party. Half (53%) used four or more drugs.

A study of rave attenders in Chicago found that 48.9% had used any club drugs, 29.8% used LSD, 27.7% ecstasy and 8.5% methamphetamine. Rave attenders used club drugs with other drugs such as marijuana (87%), alcohol (65.2%) and cocaine/crack (26.1%).

What Is the Risk?

There are many negative physical and psychological side effects of club drugs. The reason club drugs present a potential HIV risk is because they can lower inhibitions, impair judgment, increase sexual endurance and encourage sexual risk-taking. With injected drugs, there is also a potential risk from sharing injection equipment.

The risk for HIV occurs mainly when drug use occurs during sexual activity. For example, methamphetamine is often used to initiate, enhance and prolong sexual encounters, allowing individuals to have sexual intercourse with numerous partners. Poppers are used for receptive anal sex, to relax the anal sphincter. Speed is also dehydrating, which may make men and women more prone to tears in the anus, vagina or mouth, and therefore more prone to HIV/STD [sexually transmitted disease] infections.

In one study, HIV–[negative] heterosexual methamphetamine users reported an average of 9.4 sex partners over two months. The number of unprotected sexual acts in two months averaged 21.5 for vaginal sex, 6.3 for anal sex and 41.7 for oral sex. Most users (86%) reported engaging in "marathon sex" while high on methamphetamine. Over one-third (37%) of users reported injecting, and of those, almost half had shared and/or borrowed needles.

Unprotected sex with a partner whose HIV status is unknown is a high-risk activity. A survey of gay men found that

21% of HIV+ [positive] and 9% of HIV–men reported unprotected anal sex with a partner of unknown status at their most recent circuit party.

A study of gay men at raves in New York City found that about one-third (34%) used ecstasy at least once a month. Men who used ecstasy were more likely to report recent unprotected anal intercourse than men who used other drugs, including alcohol.

Why Do People Use Club Drugs?

For many people, straight or gay, drug use and sex are a natural occurrence at raves and circuit parties, and one of the appeals of these parties. These parties are popular social activities for some groups of youth and gay men, and there can be strong peer pressure to use drugs and be sexually active. While circuit parties and raves may not themselves cause drug use, they may attract persons who are more inclined to use drugs.

People use club drugs for many reasons. Some people use club drugs to have fun, dance and loosen inhibitions. Others use them to escape their problems and to counter feelings of depression or anxiety. Parental drug use, childhood sexual abuse and depression are some of the factors that may lead to drug use.

What's Being Done?

A drug treatment program for gay methamphetamine users in Los Angeles, CA, sought to reduce drug use and HIV-related sexual risk behaviors. Treatment options included: 1) cognitive behavioral therapy, a 90-minute group session delivered three times a week; 2) contingency management, a behavioral intervention that offered increasingly valuable vouchers for abstinence from drug use; and 3) cognitive behavioral therapy culturally tailored to gay issues. All men reduced their drug use, and those using contingency management reduced drug use longer. The highest reduction in sexual risk-taking occurred in men who used the culturally tailored program.

DanceSafe promotes health and safety within the rave and nightclub community, with local chapters throughout the US and Canada. DanceSafe trains volunteers to be health educators and drug abuse prevention counselors at raves and nightclubs. They use a harm reduction approach and primarily target non-addicted, recreational drug users. DanceSafe offers information on drugs, safer sex and staying healthy, and in some venues offers pill testing to make sure drugs do not contain harmful substitutes.

Twelve Step programs such as Crystal Meth Anonymous (CMA), Narcotics Anonymous (NA) and Alcoholics Anonymous (AA) are for people for whom drug use has become a problem. Twelve Step advocates abstinence from crystal meth, alcohol and other illicit drugs. Twelve Step meetings occur in many cities across the US.

The PROTECT project at the South Florida Regional Prevention Center aims to reduce club-drug use among young gay men. PROTECT trains police officers, teachers and other community stakeholders on club drugs, particularly ecstacy. They also developed a web site with a chat room monitored by peer counselors.

Stepping Stone, in San Diego, CA, is a residential drug treatment facility for gay men and lesbians. Most of their clients are poly drug users and most are dually diagnosed with psychiatric disorders. They address sexual behaviors and mental health issues in the context of drug abuse treatment. Stepping Stone sponsors a harm reduction social marketing campaign to increase awareness of the dangers of club drugs and alcohol.

What Needs to Be Done?

Several organizations are currently addressing the negative effects of club drugs at raves and parties across the country. More education is needed about the toxicity of club drugs, poly drug use and the connection between drug use and unsafe sex. Referrals for mental health counseling should also be made available at these venues.

The gay community needs to address the very real pressures in some sub-communities to party and be highly sexually active, and ask the question "is drug use worth the risks men are taking?" It is not enough to attempt to reduce drug use and abuse at circuit parties without also addressing the powerful sexual motivations to using drugs.

When prescribing Viagra, physicians should counsel men on safer sex and the harmful effects of combining Viagra with methamphetamines, poppers and ecstasy. Physicians should inquire about club drug use among their HIV+ patients and counsel them on the danger of combining them with HIV treatment drugs. Physicians should be aware that club drug use can affect adherence to HIV drugs.

6

The Recreational Use of Ecstasy Is Harmful

National Institute on Drug Abuse (NIDA)

Established in 1974, the National Institute on Drug Abuse (NIDA) is a federal institute specializing in drug abuse research for public education, drug abuse prevention and treatment, and policymaking.

Ecstasy or MDMA (methylenedioxymethamphetamine) is a club drug used at raves and nightclubs for its stimulant and psyche-delic effects. Recreational use of this substance has various harm-ful short-term and long-term consequences, the latter of which have been demonstrated in scientific studies. Among its undesir-able immediate effects (e.g., nausea, jaw-clenching), ecstasy users face several dangers: ecstasy may be adulterated with other illicit drugs, such as cocaine; users may overdose, leading to panic at-tacks, high blood pressure, or seizures; and vigorous physical ac-tivity on ecstasy has resulted in deadly cases of serotonin syn-drome, in which the body heats up to lethal temperatures. Beside addiction, the potential long-term effects include impairments to memory, attention, and mood. This necessitates more research on the drug as well increasing awareness of ecstasy's dangers and deterring abuse.

MDMA is an illegal drug that acts as both a stimulant and psychedelic, producing an energizing effect, as well as distortions in time and perception and enhanced enjoy-ment from tactile experiences. Typically, MDMA (an acronym

National Institute on Drug Abuse (NIDA), "MDMA (Ecstasy) Abuse," in NIDA.NIH. Gov, March 2006, pp. 1-7.

for its chemical name 3,4-methylenedioxymethamphetamine) is taken orally, usually in a tablet or capsule, and its effects last approximately 3 to 6 hours. The average reported dose is one to two tablets, with each tablet typically containing between 60 and 120 milligrams of MDMA. It is not uncommon for users to take a second dose of the drug as the effects of the first dose begin to fade.

Researchers have determined that many ecstasy tablets contain not only MDMA but also a number of other drugs or drug combinations that can be harmful as well.

MDMA can affect the brain by altering the activity of chemical messengers, or neurotransmitters, which enable nerve cells in the brain to communicate with one another. Research in animals has shown that MDMA in moderate to high doses can be toxic to nerve cells that contain serotonin and can cause long-lasting damage to them. Furthermore, MDMA raises body temperature. On rare but largely unpredictable occasions, this has led to severe medical consequences, including death. Also, MDMA causes the release of another neurotransmitter, norepinephrine, which is likely the cause of the increase in heart rate and blood pressure that often accompanies MDMA use.

Although MDMA is known universally among users as ecstasy, researchers have determined that many ecstasy tablets contain not only MDMA but also a number of other drugs or drug combinations that can be harmful as well. Adulterants found in MDMA tablets purchased on the street include methamphetamine, caffeine, the over-the-counter cough suppressant dextromethorphan, the diet drug ephedrine, and cocaine. Also, as with many other drugs of abuse, MDMA is rarely used alone. It is not uncommon for users to mix MDMA with other substances, such as alcohol and marijuana.

A Brief History of MDMA

MDMA was developed in Germany in the early 1900s as a parent compound to be used to synthesize other pharmaceuticals. During the 1970s, in the United States, some psychiatrists began using MDMA as a psychotherapeutic tool, despite the fact that the drug had never undergone formal clinical trials nor received approval from the U.S. Food and Drug Administration (FDA) for use in humans. In fact, it was only in late 2000 that the FDA approved the first small clinical trial for MDMA that will determine if the drug can be used safely with 2 sessions of ongoing psychotherapy under carefully monitored conditions to treat post-traumatic stress disorder. Nevertheless, the drug gained a small following among psychiatrists in the late 1970s and early 1980s, with some even calling it "penicillin for the soul" because it was perceived to enhance communication in patient sessions and reportedly allowed users to achieve insights about their problems. It was also during this time that MDMA first started becoming available on the street. In 1985, the U.S. Drug Enforcement Administration (DEA) banned the drug, placing it on its list of Schedule I drugs, corresponding to those substances with no proven therapeutic value.

What Is the Scope of MDMA Abuse in the U.S.?

It is difficult to determine the exact scope of this problem because MDMA is often used in combination with other substances, and does not appear in some traditional data sources, such as treatment admission rates.

More than 11 million persons aged 12 or older reported using ecstasy at least once in their lifetimes, according to the 2004 National Survey on Drug Use and Health. The number of current (use in past month) users in 2004 was estimated to be 450,000.

The Drug Abuse Warning Network, maintained by the Substance Abuse and Mental Health Services Administration, reported that mentions of MDMA in drug abuse-related cases in hospital emergency departments were 2,221 for the third and fourth quarters of 2003. The majority of patients who came to emergency departments mentioning MDMA as a factor in their admissions during that time were aged 18–20.

There is, however, some encouraging news from NIDA's [National Institute for Drug Abuse] Monitoring the Future (MTF) survey, an annual survey used to track drug abuse trends among adolescents in middle and high schools across the country. Between 2001 and 2005, annual ecstasy use decreased by 52 percent in 8th-graders, 58 percent in 10th-graders, and 67 percent in 12th-graders. Rates of lifetime MDMA use decreased significantly from 2004 to 2005 among 12th-graders.

In 2005, 8th-graders reported a significant decrease in perceived harmfulness in using MDMA occasionally. The MTF data also show that MDMA use extends across many demographic subgroups. Among 12th-graders in 2005, for example, 3.9 percent of Whites, 3.0 percent of Hispanic students, and 1.4 percent of African-Americans reported using MDMA in the year prior to the survey.

Who Is Abusing MDMA?

MDMA first gained popularity among adolescents and young adults in the nightclub scene or weekend-long dance parties known as raves. However, the profile of the typical MDMA user has been changing. Community-level data from NIDA's Community Epidemiology Work Group (CEWG), continued to report that use of MDMA has spread among populations outside the nightclub scene.

Reports also indicate that use is spreading beyond predominantly White youth to a broader range of ethnic groups. In Chicago, the drug continues to be predominantly used by

White youth, but there are increasing reports of its use by African-American adults in their twenties and thirties. Also, indicators in New York suggest that both the distribution and use of club drugs are becoming more common in non-White communities.

Other NIDA research shows that MDMA has also become a popular drug among urban gay males. Reports have shown that some gay and bisexual men take MDMA and other club drugs in myriad venues. This is concerning given that the use of club drugs has been linked to high-risk sexual behaviors that may lead to HIV or other sexually transmitted diseases. Many gay males in big cities report using MDMA as part of a multiple-drug experience that includes marijuana, cocaine, methamphetamine, ketamine, and other legal and illegal substances.

Over the course of a week following moderate use of the drug, many MDMA users report feeling a range of emotions . . . as severe as true clinical depression.

What Are the Effects of MDMA?

MDMA has become a popular drug, in part because of the positive effects that a person may experience within an hour or so after taking a single dose. Those effects include feelings of mental stimulation, emotional warmth, empathy toward others, a general sense of well-being, and decreased anxiety. In addition, users report enhanced sensory perception as a hallmark of the MDMA experience. Because of the drug's stimulant properties, when used in club or dance settings, MDMA can also enable users to dance for extended periods. However, there are some users who report undesirable effects immediately, including anxiety, agitation, and recklessness.

As noted, MDMA is not a benign drug. MDMA can produce a variety of adverse health effects, including nausea, chills, sweating, involuntary teeth clenching, muscle cramping, and blurred vision. MDMA overdose can also occur—the symptoms can include high blood pressure, faintness, panic attacks, and in severe cases, a loss of consciousness and seizures.

Because of its stimulant properties and the environments in which it is often taken, MDMA is associated with vigorous physical activity for extended periods. This can lead to one of the most significant, although rare, acute adverse effects—a marked rise in body temperature (hyperthermia). Treatment of hyperthermia requires prompt medical attention, as it can rapidly lead to muscle breakdown, which can in turn result in kidney failure. In addition, dehydration, hypertension, and heart failure may occur in susceptible individuals. MDMA can also reduce the pumping efficiency of the heart, of particular concern during periods of increased physical activity, further complicating these problems.

MDMA is rapidly absorbed into the human bloodstream, but once in the body, MDMA metabolites interfere with the body's ability to metabolize, or break down, the drug. As a result, additional doses of MDMA can produce unexpectedly high blood levels, which could worsen the cardiovascular and other toxic effects of this drug. MDMA also interferes with the metabolism of other drugs, including some of the adulterants that may be found in MDMA tablets. In the hours after taking the drug, MDMA produces significant reductions in mental abilities. These changes, particularly those affecting memory, can last for up to a week, and possibly longer in regular users. The fact that MDMA markedly impairs information processing emphasizes the potential dangers of performing complex or skilled activities, such as driving a car, while under the influence of this drug.

Over the course of a week following moderate use of the drug, many MDMA users report feeling a range of emotions, including anxiety, restlessness, irritability, and sadness that in some individuals can be as severe as true clinical depression. Similarly, elevated anxiety, impulsiveness, and aggression, as well as sleep disturbances, lack of appetite, and reduced interest in and pleasure from sex have been observed in regular MDMA users. Some of these disturbances may not be directly attributable to MDMA, but may be related to some of the other drugs often used in combination with MDMA, such as cocaine or marijuana, or to adulterants commonly found in MDMA tablets.

What Does MDMA Do to the Brain?

MDMA affects the brain by increasing the activity of at least three neurotransmitters (the chemical messengers of brain cells): serotonin, dopamine, and norepinephrine. Like other amphetamines, MDMA causes these neurotransmitters to be released from their storage sites in neurons, resulting in increased neurotransmitter activity. Compared to the very potent stimulant, methamphetamine, MDMA causes greater serotonin release and somewhat lesser dopamine release. Serotonin is a neurotransmitter that plays an important role in the regulation of mood, sleep, pain, appetite, and other behaviors. The excess release of serotonin by MDMA likely causes the mood-elevating effects experienced by MDMA users. However, by releasing large amounts of serotonin, MDMA causes the brain to become significantly depleted of this important neurotransmitter, contributing to the negative behavioral aftereffects that users often experience for several days after taking MDMA.

Numerous studies in animals have demonstrated that MDMA can damage serotonin-containing neurons; some of these studies have shown these effects to be long lasting. This suggests that such damage may occur in humans as well; however, measuring serotonin damage in humans is more difficult. Studies have shown that some heavy MDMA users experience long-lasting confusion, depression, and selective impairment of working memory and attention processes. Such memory impairments have been associated with a decrease in serotonin metabolites or other markers of serotonin function. Imaging studies in MDMA users have shown changes in brain activity in regions involved in cognition, emotion, and motor function. However, improved imaging technologies and more research are needed to confirm these findings and to elucidate the exact nature of the effects of MDMA on the human brain.

It is also important to keep in mind that many users of ecstasy may unknowingly be taking other drugs that are sold as ecstasy, and/or they may intentionally use other drugs, such as marijuana, which could contribute to these behavioral effects. Additionally, most studies in people do not have behavioral measures from before the users began taking drugs, making it difficult to rule out pre-existing conditions. Factors such as gender, dosage, frequency and intensity of use, age at which use began, the use of other drugs, as well as genetic and environmental factors all may play a role in some of the cognitive deficits that result from MDMA use and should be taken into consideration when studying the effects of MDMA in humans.

Experiments have shown that animals prefer MDMA, much like they do cocaine, over other pleasurable stimuli, another hallmark of most addictive drugs.

Given that most MDMA users are young and in their reproductive years, it is possible that some female users may be pregnant when they take MDMA, either inadvertently or intentionally because of the misperception that it is a safe drug. The potential adverse effects of MDMA on the developing fetus are of great concern. Behavioral studies in animals have found significant adverse effects on tests of learning and memory from exposure to MDMA during a developmental period equivalent to the third trimester in humans. However, the effects of MDMA on animals earlier in development are unclear; therefore, more research is needed to determine what the effects of MDMA are on the developing human nervous system.

Is MDMA Addictive?

For some people, MDMA can be addictive. A survey of young adult and adolescent MDMA users found that 43 percent of those who reported ecstasy use met the accepted diagnostic criteria for dependence, as evidenced by continued use despite knowledge of physical or psychological harm, withdrawal effects, and tolerance (or diminished response), and 34 percent met the criteria for drug abuse. Almost 60 percent of people who use MDMA report withdrawal symptoms, including fatigue, loss of appetite, depressed feelings, and trouble concentrating.

MDMA affects many of the same neurotransmitter systems in the brain that are targeted by other addictive drugs. Experiments have shown that animals prefer MDMA, much like they do cocaine, over other pleasurable stimuli, another hallmark of most addictive drugs.

What Do We Know About Preventing MDMA Abuse?

Because social context and networks seem to be an important component of MDMA use, the use of peer-led advocacy and drug prevention programs may be a promising approach to reduce MDMA use among adolescents and young adults. High schools and colleges can serve as important venues for delivering messages about the effects of MDMA use. Providing accurate scientific information regarding the effects of MDMA is important if we hope to reduce the damaging effects of this drug. Education is one of the most important tools for use in preventing MDMA abuse.

Are There Effective Treatments for MDMA Abuse?

There are no specific treatments for MDMA abuse. The most effective treatments for drug abuse and addiction are cognitive behavioral interventions that are designed to help modify the patient's thinking, expectancies, and behaviors, and to increase skills in coping with life's stressors. Drug abuse recovery support groups may be effective in combination with behavioral interventions to support long-term, drug-free recovery. There are currently no pharmacological treatments for dependence on MDMA.

7

The Harm of Ecstasy Has Been Misrepresented by Researchers and Reporters

Ilsa Jerome

Ilsa Jerome is a research and information specialist at the Multidisciplinary Association for Psychedelic Studies (MAPS), a research and educational organization that sponsors clinical studies designed to obtain approval from the Food and Drug Administration (FDA) for the use of ecstasy as a prescription medicine.

The media coverage on studies claiming that ecstasy causes injury to the brain—as well as researchers' positions on their own findings—are frequently misleading. Statements that the drug harms the brains of first-time users and results in memory loss cannot be supported by published reports and presentations delivered at conferences. For instance, in light of a new ecstasy study, news articles commented on the possible harms of taking the drug. However, an examination of the published findings and conference presentations shows that the casual use of ecstasy may not create memory deficits, decrease serotonin, and that, although ecstasy users were more impulsive than nonusers, they exhibited less depressive symptoms. Confronting misrepresentations in the media on the latest ecstasy studies is an invitation to track down the original research and make one's own judgment.

Ilsa Jerome, "Report on Third Prospective Study of Ecstasy Users: Examining Attention and Memory," Maps.org, June 2007. Reproduced by permission.

The *Archives of General Psychiatry* has just published the latest in a series of reports from the Netherlands XTC Toxicity (or NeXT) research team comparing cognitive function in ecstasy users and non-ecstasy using controls before and after they used ecstasy. The study is the third prospective study from this team, but it is the first to examine attention and memory beyond assessing working memory. In contrast with earlier publications, this report describes finding differences between the two groups, with ecstasy-nave controls performing better verbal memory tasks at follow-up than ecstasy users.

While these findings are notable as the first from a prospective study, there are problems in the analysis and presentation of the data that raise questions about the meaning and significance of study results. Perhaps the greatest problem with the findings relates to whether the researchers performed appropriate analyses for the comparisons they wished to make. However, other issues include retaining apparent outliers in the data, interpretation of results and overstating the significance of their conclusions.

The researchers began the study by recruiting people who planned on using ecstasy in the future, giving them tests of attention, verbal and visual memory before any of them had used any ecstasy. Up to three years after the first time, at a point when a number of people had started using ecstasy, the researchers gave participants the same tests of attention and memory. These participants included 59 people who said they had started using ecstasy and 61 who said they had not used it yet, with the controls matched on the basis of age and estimated verbal IQ. The ecstasy users reported taking an average of 3.2 tablets (range = 0.5–30 tablets, median = 1.5 tablets). Both groups performed similarly on these tests prior to anyone using ecstasy. The researchers subtracted the first score from the second score and compared the resulting change scores, finding that in most cases, ecstasy users and people who had not used ecstasy performed similarly on tests of attention and memory. However, non-ecstasy users had higher change scores on immediate and delayed recall on a list-learning task. Cumulative ecstasy dose, but not duration of use, was associated with differences in delayed recall and recognition of word lists. The researchers also found that past cocaine and amphetamine use was associated with differences in delayed list recall. After controlling for amphetamine and cocaine use, the researchers still found an association between cumulative ecstasy dose and recognition, but not delayed recall. The researchers interpreted their findings as indicating that even a relatively low dose of ecstasy can affect verbal memory.

This research team has even presented data indicating that low dose ecstasy had no effects on estimated numbers of serotonin uptake sites.

Before going any further into these findings, it should be noted that everyone in this study attained scores within the normal range, and that in this case, relatively low use includes using 30 tablets. This being the case, the finding do not support claims that one or two doses of ecstasy impair verbal memory.

However, there are a number of reasons for not accepting the results at face value.

First of all, despite referring to detecting a decline in verbal memory, the researchers did not perform analyses comparing memory and attention before and after ecstasy use for each group as well as differences in performance over time in each group. Using change scores instead of raw scores creates a situation where improvement and impairment can look the same. And this is in fact what happened in the study; ecstasy user scores before and after their starting ecstasy use were for the most part similar. In some cases they were lower, and in others, they were higher. People who had not used ecstasy had higher verbal memory performance scores when tested again while ecstasy users scores were either the same or only slightly lower.

In an earlier report, the same team of researchers excluded a participant who had used 20 tablets from their prospective study of changes in brain activity during a working memory task (Jager et al. 2007). In that study, the researchers performed analyses with and without that participant, finding marginal effects when they included this person. Thus it is surprising that the researchers did not apply the same restrictions in this study or compare analyses with and without people who used 20 or more tablets. It is possible that removing people reporting use of 20 or more ecstasy tablets from the sample would not have found significant differences in verbal memory change scores. The researchers do not even state how many people reported used greater than ten tablets, despite using this amount as a limit in earlier studies.

The authors already address some of the other confounds and problems in their study in the Discussion section, even acknowledging that ecstasy users still reported greater use of other substances and noting that medical and neuropsychiatric history were determined on the basis of self-report only. It also remains unclear as to the degree that people who used ecstasy were unintentionally exposed to amphetamine or methamphetamine sold either alone or along with MDMA as ecstasy. The authors note that previous studies have failed to find any changes in verbal memory in low to moderate users, attributing the failure to those studies having smaller sample sizes. However, this explanation does not address studies that failed to find any effects of ecstasy use on memory, even when other effects were found (for instance Simon and Mattick. 2002; Halpern et al. 2004). They note that providing all participants with information on the risks of ecstasy may have created a self-fulfilling prophecy wherein ecstasy users did less well because of worries that they might confirm stereotypes about ecstasy users (Cole et al. 2006), but dismiss this possibility by stating that they did not see the effect in the whole sample. However, as only those who knew they had started using ecstasy would be vulnerable to the effects of stereotype threat, it remains possible that non-users performed better because they were not worried that they would do badly.

However, above and beyond the issues described above, the authors overstate and even misrepresent what their findings mean. As already noted, they describe significant differences in change scores as a decline in ecstasy users verbal memory throughout much of the paper, though at the beginning of the discussion they acknowledge that what they found was improvement in non-ecstasy users verbal memory. They suggest that the main underlying factor for their findings must be serotonin depletion in ecstasy users, yet when taken together, previous studies do not support a relationship between changes in the serotonin systems and impaired cognitive function in ecstasy users (Cowan 2006). Previous prospective reports from the same team and using a similar (but apparently not identical) sample failed to find signs of neuronal injury or damage or changes in brain activity or changes in task performance on a working memory task (de Win et al. 2006). This research team has even presented data indicating that low dose ecstasy had no effects on estimated numbers of serotonin uptake sites. It is notable that a recent study of the effects of the selective serotonin uptake inhibitor (SSRI) escitalopram alone or combined with a 5HT1A antagonist (pindolol) or a 5HT2A antagonist (ketanserin) in healthy drug-nave people found that the SSRI alone impaired verbal memory in health participants, and that the 5HT1A antagonist caused a further decline (Wingen et al. 2006). If these results are confirmed in other studies, it suggests that even when it is seen, impaired verbal memory in ecstasy users need not be the result of serotonin neurotoxicity but may occur as a result of downregulation of specific serotonin receptors. Finally, while ecstasy users in this [study] reported considerably lower lifetime ecstasy use than seen in retrospective or longitudinal reports of ecstasy users, the inclusion of at least one person reporting use of 30 tablets means that the data may not represent the effects of low lifetime ecstasy use.

Notes

Cole JC, Michailidou K, Jerome L, Sumnall HR. (2006) Abstract The effects of sterotype threat on cognitive function in ecstasy users. J Psychopharmacol;20: 518–525. http://www.maps.org/sys/w3pb.pl?mode=search&c_pkey=22728&displayformat=allinfo&type=citation

Cowan RL. (2007) Neuroimaging research in human MDMA users: a review. Psychopharmacology (Berl). 2007 Jan; 189:539–556. http://www.maps.org/sys/w3pb.pl?mode=search&c_pkey=22836&displayformat=allinfo&type=citation

de Win MM, Reneman L, Jager G, Vlieger EJ, Olabarriaga SD, Lavini C, Bisschops I, Majoie CB, Booij J, den Heeten GJ, van den Brink W. (2007) A prospective cohort study on sustained effects of low-dose ecstasy use on the brain in new ecstasy users. Neuropsychopharmacology. 32(2): 458–470. Epub 2006 Nov 1. http://www.maps.org/sys/w3pb.pl?mode=search&c_pkey22871&displayformat=allinfo&type=citation

Halpern JH, Pope HG, Sherwood AR, Barry S, Hudson JH, Yurgelun-Todd D. (2004) Residual neuropsychological effects of illicit 3.4-methylenedioxymethamphetamine (MDMA) in individuals with minimal exposure to other drugs. Drug Alcohol Depend 75: 135–147. http://www.maps.org/sys/w3pb.pl?mode=search&c_pkey=20587&displayformat=allinfo&type=citation

Jager G, de Win MM, Vervaeke HK, Schilt T, Kahn RS, van den Brink W, van Ree JM, Ramsey NF. (2007A) Incidental use of ecstasy: no evidence for harmful effects on cognitive brain function in a prospective fMRI study. Psychopharmacology (Berl). May 3; [Epub ahead of print] http://www.maps.org/sys/w3pb.pl?mode=search&c_pkey=22906&displayformat=allinfo&type=citation

Schlit T, de Win MM, Koeter M, Jager G, Korf DJ, van den Brink W, Schmand B. (2007) Cognition in novice ecstasy users with minimal exposure to other drugs: a prospective cohort study. Arch Gen Psychiatry 64: 728–736. http://www.maps.org/sys/w3pb.pl?mode=search&c_pkey=22908&displayformat=allinfo&type=citation

Simon NG, Mattick RP. (2002) The impact of regular Ecstasy use on memory function. Addiction 97:1523–1529. http://www.maps.org/sys/w3pb.pl?mode=search&c_pkey=5577&displayformat=allinfo&type=citation

Wingen M, Kuypers KP, Ramaekers JG. (2006) Selective verbal and spatial memory impairment after 5-HT1A and 5-HT2A receptor blockade in healthy volunteers pretreated with an SSRI.J Psychopharmacol [Epub ahead of print]

8

The Recreational Use of Ecstasy Can Destroy Lives

Karen de Seve

Karen de Seve is a contributor to the Weekly Reader publication Current Health 2.

Although the first time can seem incredible, using ecstasy is not a trivial matter. Users are drawn to the way it makes them feel temporarily, but the side effects can be very dangerous and even deadly. Even just one use of ecstasy can drain the brain of serotonin, which can result in a crash from happiness to depression. Extended users of ecstasy can become moody and forgetful, or suffer from permanent depression. Ecstasy can also be a gateway to crime and other drugs, such as marijuana and heroin.

The first time Jimmy Gatehouse tried Ecstasy, he wasn't sure what to expect. "I first used it when I was 15," he says. "I took just one pill, and I didn't feel anything. So I bought another one, and about half an hour later, I was fascinated at everything. It was insane." Little did Gatehouse know that three years later a judge would order him to go into a rehabilitation program to kick the habit.

Now 18, Gatehouse says he used to go out of his way to buy Ecstasy pills—or "beans" as they are also known on the street—in his hometown of Portland, Maine. "I'd do it before I'd go to clubs," he says. At 16, Gatehouse stopped going to school and did the drug for 30 days in a row. "School was calling my house, but my mother was always working, so I'd just make up excuses and lie to my mother. My grades were poor."

When Ecstasy (clinically known as 3–4 methylene-dioxymethamphetamine, or MDMA) wasn't available, Gatehouse turned to alcohol and marijuana. Sometimes he would trade drinks or cigarettes for pills. Other times, Gatehouse hankered for MDMA so much that he committed robbery and assault to get money to buy the pills. "I'd be drinking, and I'd go steal money, or I'd beat someone up for money so I could go buy drugs," he told Current Health 2, explaining that he was arrested and put on probation by the county court. When his urine tests revealed that Gatehouse was still drinking and taking drugs, the court sent him to a six-month rehabilitation program at Phoenix House in Auburn, Maine.

Hooked on a Feeling

What drew Gatehouse to MDMA time and again was the way it temporarily made him feel. "It alters the chemistry of the brain," says Dr. Glen Hanson, a professor of pharmacology and toxicology at the University of Utah, who has studied the drug since the early 1980s. That's when MDMA first appeared in the United States. "If you look at something, it may become distorted or a different color. Sound and the sense[s] of touch, taste, and smell might be enhanced."

The resulting feelings of depression can last for several years, if not permanently, and users became moody and forgetful.

Users like Gatehouse crave those temporary feel-good sensations—good mood and pleasures—that MDMA unlocks in the brain. But there are after effects to the drug-induced happiness. Gatehouse remembers getting agitated and grinding his teeth the first time he took Ecstasy. Other reactions can include sweating, fatigue, muscle spasms, severe thirst, a racing heart rate, and a swift rise in body temperature, called hyperthermia. Those who combine MDMA with the physical exertion of fast dancing are particularly at risk for hyperthermia because the drug interferes with the brain's ability to control body temperature. "This is not a trivial drug," says Hanson. "It has severe risk associated with its recreational use. People have died from it."

Ecstasy and the Brain

Ecstasy signals nerve cells in the brain to release two brain chemicals: serotonin and dopamine. Serotonin plays a role in how the brain regulates perception, mood, memory, emotions, and sleep. Dopamine triggers the brain to perceive pleasure and reward, and it is involved with decision making and movement.

Taking just one high dose of MDMA—which has a chemical structure similar to methamphetamines—can drain the brain of serotonin. That's because the drug signals serotonin-producing cells to fire over and over until the nerve cells can't make serotonin fast enough. When that happens, the user usually crashes from a happy high and swings to the other end of the emotional spectrum: depression. Extended use damages the serotonin-producing cells so they can no longer tell the brain to feel happy. The resulting feelings of depression can last for several years, if not permanently, and users became moody and forgetful.

Gatehouse felt that way after his month-long MDMA binge. "I stopped doing it because I wasn't thinking right," he recalls. "After a few weeks I did another pill, but I slowed down to two or three every couple of months. That's when I started smoking weed and drinking heavily."

"Ecstasy tends to be more of a weekend party drug than a daily-use drug like methamphetamine," says Dr. James Mulligan, the medical director at Seabrook House rehabilitation center in Bridgeton, N.J. He says the number of MDMA users in treatment has dropped in recent years, but most teens who have come to his clinic are multidrug users. Mulligan has also seen patients who started out on MDMA but then moved to other substances. "Ecstasy is a gate-opening drug, and that is risky stuff," he explains. "Once you learn how to get one drug, then you get into that groupie thing and are exposed to other drugs, such as heroin."

Worth the Price?

Ecstasy isn't cheap. Gatehouse paid $15 to $20 for a single-dose pill. Double and triple "stacked" pills would cost $25 or more. "The dealer would name the price depending on the strength," recalls Gatehouse. "But the kind didn't really matter; I'd buy it anyway."

Gatehouse paid a lot more than cash for his cravings, and so did the people he assaulted and robbed to get MDMA money. After his six months at Phoenix House, he'll enter an after-care program and move back in with his mother in Portland. He's lucky to have a job at a local restaurant waiting for him when he returns. From there he plans to apply to college.

Gatehouse wants other teens to hear his message about Ecstasy: "Don't do it. It damages your brain and messes with your body," he says. "I'll never do it again."

9

The Psychiatric Use of Ecstasy Can Help Heal Psychological Trauma

Amy Turner

A journalist, Amy Turner has written for the United Kingdom's Times *and* Sunday Times.

Ecstasy (MDMA) is known at nightclubs and raves as the "love drug"; pure MDMA creates feelings of euphoria, trust, and openness. For posttraumatic stress disorder (PTSD), the trust and openness that ecstasy produces may be the key to successful treatment. Systematic, supervised clinical trials have shown that MDMA lowers the defenses of PTSD sufferers, allowing them to relive and face the trauma of rape, violence, or abuse without becoming retraumatized or repressing emotions, which is a primary step in overcoming the debilitating emotional disorder. Such anecdotal evidence demonstrates that the drug can be of great value in psychotherapy. But its notorious reputation and cultural associations—sparked by its illegal use at raves and several high-profile ecstasy deaths—are obstacles to further research and approval of MDMA as a therapeutic drug.

An Ecstasy tablet. That's what it took to make Donna Kilgore feel alive again—that and the doctor who prescribed it. As the pill began to take effect, she giggled for the first time in ages. She felt warm and fuzzy, as if she was floating. The anxiety melted away. Gradually, it all became clear: the guilt, the anger, the shame.

Before, she'd been frozen, unable to feel anything but fear for 10 years. Touching her own arms was, she says, "like touching a corpse". She was terrified, unable to respond to her loving husband or rock her baby to sleep. She couldn't drive over bridges for fear of dying, was by turns uncontrollably angry and paralysed with numbness. When she spoke, she heard her voice as if it were miles away; her head felt detached from her body. "It was like living in a movie but watching myself through the camera lens," she says. "I wasn't real."

Unknowingly, Donna, now 39, had post-traumatic stress disorder (PTSD). And she would become the first subject in a pioneering American research programme to test the effects of MDMA—otherwise known as the dancefloor drug Ecstasy—on PTSD sufferers.

Some doctors believe MDMA could be the key to solving previously untreatable deep-rooted traumas. For a hard core of PTSD cases, no amount of antidepressants or psychotherapy can rid them of the horror of systematic abuse or a bad near-death experience, and the slightest reminder triggers vivid flashbacks.

PTSD-specific psychotherapy has always been based on the idea that the sufferer must be guided back to the pivotal moment of that trauma—the crash, the battlefield, the moment of rape—and relive it before they can move on and begin to heal. But what if that trauma is insurmountable? What if a person is so horrified by their experience that even to think of revisiting it can bring on hysterics? The Home Office estimates that 11,000 clubbers take Ecstasy every weekend. Could MDMA—the illegal class-A rave drug, found in the system of Leah Betts when she died in 1995, and over 200 others since—really help? Dr Michael Mithoefer, the psychiatrist from South Carolina who struggled for years to get funding and permission for the study, believes so. Some regard his study—approved by the US government—as irresponsible, dangerous even. But Mithoefer's results tell a different story.

Therapeutic Potential and Criminalization

MDMA was patented in 1912 by the German pharmaceutical company Merck. To begin with, it was merely an intermediate chemical used in creating a drug to control bleeding. In the 1920s MDMA was used in studies on blood glucose as a substitute for adrenaline. The Merck chemist Max Oberlin concluded that it would be worth "keeping an eye on this field". Still, no further studies were carried out until 1952, when the chemist Dr Albert van Schoor tested the toxicity of MDMA on flies. "Flies lie in supine position, then death," he recorded.

MDMA's therapeutic potential wasn't realised until 1976, when the American chemist Alexander Shulgin tried it on himself. He noted that its effect, "an easily controlled altered state of consciousness with emotional and sensual overtones", could be ideal for psychotherapy, as it induced a state of openness and trust without hallucination or paranoia. It quickly became known as a wonder drug, and began to be used widely in couples therapy and for treating anxiety disorders. None of these tests was "empirical" in the scientific sense—no placebos, no follow-up testing—but anecdotally the results were almost entirely positive.

Has MDMA's reputation been tarnished so badly that its potential medical value has been overshadowed?

Word, and supplies, of the new "love drug" got out, and in the early 1980s it became popular in the fashionable clubs of Dallas, LA and London, where it was known as Ecstasy, X or "dolphins". As use became widespread, the US authorities panicked, and by 1985 MDMA was an illegal, schedule-1 drug. UK laws were even tighter: MDMA, illegal under the 1971 Misuse of Drugs Act, was categorised class A in 1977, carrying a sentence of up to seven years for possession.

Criminalisation put [an end] to MDMA research almost overnight, at least until Mithoefer's current programme began.

But it didn't stop the ravers. The drug was popular in the late 1980s and early 1990s for its energising, euphoric effects. There are no official figures for that period, but the Home Office estimates that in 2006/7, between 236,000 and 341,000 people took Ecstasy. Experts say the drug is far less fashionable now than in its heyday in 1988, the second so-called "summer of love".

The MDMA used in the studies—the drug Dr Mithoefer gave Donna and other patients—was the pure chemical compound, not the black-market Ecstasy bought by recreational users. "A lot of Ecstasy pills aren't MDMA at all," says Steve Rolles of the drug-policy reform group Transform. "They may be amphetamines, or unknown pharmaceuticals, or they can be cut with almost any drug in pill or powder form. That's when you magnify risks associated with taking a drug that's already toxic. Plus, people use it irresponsibly, mixing it with other drugs, not drinking enough water or drinking too much."

The images of Leah Betts and Lorna Spinks lying in hospital on life-support, bloodied and bloated, are familiar to all of us—we know drugs cost lives. But has MDMA's reputation been tarnished so badly that its potential medical value has been overshadowed? That question is the reason that Donna agreed to speak to the *Sunday Times* about her MDMA treatment. "It's so important people know what it did for me, what it could do for others," she says. Her voice trembles: it isn't easy to talk about what she went through.

Living Instead of Existing

In 1993, Donna was brutally raped. She was a single parent living in a small town in Alaska, working as a dental nurse for the Air Force. She was due to work an early shift the next day and her two-year-old daughter was staying with a friend for the night. She was alone at home. At midnight she opened the door to a stranger who said he was looking for his dog. He asked if her husband was at home, and a second's hesitation was enough. He burst in, backing her up against the fireplace in the living room. Donna picked up a poker to defend herself. He said: "If you co-operate, I won't kill you. I've got a gun." And he reached into his jacket.

"I dropped the poker and that was it," she says. "I thought, this is how I'm going to die. No life flashed before my eyes, I didn't think about my daughter. Just death. I left my body and I stayed that way. The next thing I remember, the cops were coming through the door with a dog."

She endured the rape with her eyes squeezed shut. That she hadn't physically struggled would later form a large part of the guilt and shame that contributed to her PTSD. "I guess a lot of women would say, 'Someone would have to kill me before I'd let that happen.' Well, I did what I thought I had to do to survive," she says. When she heard a shuffle of feet outside the door she screamed for all she was worth. Her attacker beat her. Two policemen, probably alerted by a neighbour, broke down the door and arrested the man, then drove Donna to the Air Force hospital where she worked. "Of course it was full of people who knew me," she says. "It was completely embarrassing. And after that, nobody knew what to say. People avoided me, they looked at me funny. It was miserable."

Afterwards, convinced that getting on with life was the best thing for herself and her child, Donna carried on as usual. She was embarrassed that people who knew her also knew about the rape, particularly as she was still working at the hospital. But she couldn't remember much of the attack itself, and didn't try. So she was surprised when, four years later, her symptoms started to kick in. "I had no idea it was PTSD. I couldn't understand why I was so angry, why I was having nightmares, flashbacks, fainting spells, migraine, why I felt so awful, like my body was stuffed with cotton wool. Things had been going so good."

She started drinking heavily and went from relationship to relationship, finding men hard to trust and get close to. Convinced that she was dying and wouldn't live to see her next birthday, she went to the Air Force psychiatrist. "And that's where it started—take this pill, that pill. I've been on every kind of antidepressant—Zoloft, Celexa, Lexapro, Paxil. Wellbutrin made me feel suicidal. Prozac did the same. The pills were just masking the symptoms, I wasn't getting any better."

Yet she met her "soul mate", Steve, and married him in 2000. "When I first saw him I thought, 'This is the man I'm going to spend the rest of my life with.' We were like one person, finishing each other's sentences," she says. They muddled along, with Donna putting on a brave face. She had two more children. But getting close wasn't easy: "The longer we were married, the worse I got."

Once, Steve and Donna were watching TV when she had a vivid flashback to the night she was raped. "I looked at the door, I saw it open, and that feeling came over me all over again."

I thought, 'My God, why won't this go away?' Steve tried to understand, but unless you've been through this, you don't know what it's like.

What MDMA did was clear the fog so I could see.

Donna moved to South Carolina in 2002 when Steve— also in the services—was posted there. She began seeing a psychiatrist called Dr Marcet, who diagnosed her with PTSD and attributed it to the rape. It helped to know that whatever it was had a name and a cause: "I was like, why hasn't anybody told me this before?" It was Marcet who referred her to the Mithoefers.

Donna had never taken Ecstasy before. "I was a little afraid, but I was desperate. I had to have some kind of relief. I didn't want to live any more. This was no way to wake up every morning. So I met Dr Mithoefer. I said, 'Doctor, I will do any-thing short of a lobotomy. I need to get better.'" That's how, in March 2004, Donna became the first of Mithoefer's subjects in the MDMA study. Lying on a futon, with Mithoefer on one side of her and his wife, Annie, a psychiatric nurse, on the other, talking softly to her, she swallowed the small white pill. It was her last hope.

"After 5 or 10 minutes, I started giggling and I said, 'I don't think I got the placebo,'" she recalls. "It was a fuzzy, re-laxing, on-a-different-plane feeling. Kind of floaty. It was an awakening." For the first time Donna faced her fears. "I saw myself standing on top of a mountain looking down. You know you've got to go down the mountain and up the other side to get better. But there's so much fog down there, you're afraid of going into it. You know what's down there and it's horrible."

"What MDMA did was clear the fog so I could see. Down there was guilt, anger, shame, fear. And it wasn't so bad. I thought, 'I can do this. This fear is not going to kill me.' I re-membered the rape from start to finish—those memories I had repressed so deeply." Encouraged by the Mithoefers, Donna expressed her overwhelming love for her family, how she felt protected by their support and grateful for their love.

MDMA is well known for inducing these compassionate, "loved-up" feelings. For Donna, the experience was life-changing.

So what happened when she went home? Was she cured? She sighs. "I don't know if there's such a thing as a cure. But after the first session I got up the next day and went outside, and it was like walking into a crayon box—everything was clear and bright. I did better in my job, in my marriage, with my kids. I had a feeling I'd never had before—hope. I felt I could live instead of exist."

Scrupulously Monitored

What makes MDMA so useful, Mithoefer believes, is the trust it establishes. "Many people with PTSD have a great deal of trouble trusting anybody, especially if they've been betrayed by someone who abused their trust, like a parent or a caregiver," he says. "MDMA has this effect of lowering fear and defences. It also allows more compassion for oneself and for others. People can revisit the trauma, feel the original feelings but not be retraumatised, not feel overwhelmed or have to numb out to cope with it."

Before they can take part in Mithoefer's study, every participant undergoes rigorous testing. There are 21 participants per phase and the study is now in its second phase. First, they must be diagnosed with PTSD. Then its severity is measured on the Clinician Administered PTSD Scale (Caps)—it must be at least "moderately severe". They must be "treatment-resistant", meaning they have failed to respond to at least one other type of psychotherapy and also drug treatment with an SSRI (selective serotonin reuptake inhibitor) antidepressant. They must sign a 20-page document giving informed consent; they cannot have an addiction, psychosis or bipolar disorder, because these conditions affect the ability to give consent. Then they have a physical examination, a full medical-history check and lab tests for cardiovascular disease.

There's a real difference between placebo patients and patients who got MDMA, in terms of their ability to re-live the trauma.

After the screening, the patient has two 90-minute "preparatory sessions" with the Mithoefers, to begin to build trust and get an idea of what may lie ahead. "We make sure they understand that symptoms will be stirred up, that painful feelings will come before they feel better and that they should experience them as fully as they can, and express them, rather than blocking them out," Mithoefer says. "We have one rule: during the session they don't have to talk at all if they don't want to, or they can talk about anything they feel like. But if, after an hour, the trauma topic hasn't come up, we can bring it up. But it always does come up," he chuckles.

The patient lies on the futon in the Mithoefers' living-room-style office in Charleston, South Carolina. They wear eye shades to encourage introspection, and headphones through which relaxing music is played. Annie keeps an eye on the blood-pressure cuffs and temperature gauge. Mithoefer sits opposite, taking notes. Each patient is given a recording of their session afterwards.

The patient takes either a 125mg tablet of MDMA or a placebo pill, followed by a 62.5mg dose about two hours into the therapy session. The study is double-blind, so only the emergency nurse who carries the drugs from the safe to the office knows whether the patient is getting the drug. "We can always tell whether it's real or placebo. The patient can't— some people thought they got MDMA when they didn't," says Mithoefer. "But we're seeing very encouraging results. There's a real difference between placebo patients and patients who got MDMA, in terms of their ability to relive the trauma."

Michael and Annie Mithoefer "aren't your typical kind of therapists", says Donna. She was dubious about Michael's ponytail and sandals when they first met, but she is emotional as she talks about him now. "I don't think I've ever met two people who cared so much about people getting well. I'd see tears in their eyes when I told them what I went through." Three other former patients of the Mithoefers who contacted me about this article described them as "heroes", "pioneers", even "life-savers".

At the time the Mithoefers treated Donna, in March 2004, their study had been a long time in the pipeline. Convinced of MDMA's potential, Rick Doblin, founder of the Multidisciplinary Association for Psychedelic Studies (Maps), had been in and out of the courts seeking permission from the Food & Drug Administration for clinical research since 1984. Maps, a group set up to fund psychedelic research, agreed to fund Mithoefer's study in 2000. The next year the FDA approved it. Then approval was withdrawn because of research by the neurologist George Ricuarte, at Johns Hopkins University, claiming that MDMA was lethally toxic. Even a single use, he reported, could cause brain damage and possibly Parkinson's disease. Ricuarte retracted his findings in 2002 when it turned out that bottles had been mixed up and the monkeys used as subjects had received lethal doses of methamphetamine (speed), rather than MDMA. "It was incredibly frustrating," Mithoefer says.

Mithoefer's study, which looks set to cost $1m by the time it finishes in four years' time, is scrupulously monitored. Doblin had 1,000g of MDMA made specially, each gram costing $4. Mithoefer had to obtain a licence from the Drug Enforcement Administration (DEA), which keeps track of exactly how much MDMA each licence-holder has, and periodically checks the stocks for purity. A defibrillator must be kept in the building at all times in case of cardiac arrest, and an emergency nurse must be present during the treatment session. Once the study is complete, it will be subject to peer review. Then, all being well, Mithoefer hopes to see MDMA therapy available on prescription, administered in controlled surroundings, in 5 to 10 years.

Changing Hearts and Minds

Interest is growing in the UK too, but scientists admit it will take time to change hearts and minds. Dr Ben Sessa of Bristol University's Psychopharmacology Unit has been writing papers on MDMA therapy for two years. "The Mithoefers' struggle has been ludicrous," he says. "There's plenty of anecdotal evidence that it could be really useful in psychotherapy. There they are, qualified doctors with experience and medical backup, giving people this tiny dose of MDMA with safe-guards in place. It took them 20 years for Maps to get it off the ground and it costs $1m. The irony is that thousands of people are taking this stuff every weekend and there's a 15-year-old on the street corner who'll sell it to you for a tenner."

Sessa would like to set up a programme of research in the UK, pointing to the thousands who could benefit: "For severe, unremitting PTSD sufferers, it could be a lifeline. What they're seeing in the US is people who have suffered for years sud-denly saying, 'Wow, for the first time in my life I can talk about this, I can live with it.' And these are not young ravers. They're people in their thirties, forties, fifties who have never taken drugs. It's quite remarkable."

But what about the potential for post-study abuse? Might someone who felt deflated after the elation of their MDMA session find the urge to self-medicate irresistible and pop to that 15-year-old on the corner for a quick fix? Not at all, says Sessa. "I prescribe Valium all the time, and when the course is finished the patient could go and buy Valium on the street, but they don't. Very few people are interested in recreational drugs."

I ask Donna the same question. "Would I take the drug again? Yes, definitely," she says. "But not without a therapist. It's illegal."

MDMA has been demonised.

Another former patient of Mithoefer's, a 42-year-old woman, had severe PTSD after being repeatedly and horrifi-cally beaten and locked in a basement by her father during childhood. She wished to remain anonymous because she is still in contact with her parents. When I asked her the ques-tion, she replied: "I did it to get better, not to get high. Before the treatment, I would drink to hide my symptoms. But I don't want to get drunk now, let alone take drugs. I just don't need it any more."

The harmful effects of MDMA are still under investigation. The type of research that is carried out—normally with animals or with recreational users who also take other drugs—means that the exact levels of toxicity it causes are unknown. In 2006 Dr Maartje de Win of the University of Amsterdam published research showing that Ecstasy could cause depression, anxiety and long-term memory damage after one small dose. "We really don't know how much Ecstasy affects the brain in the long term," she says. "I would be very cautious about giving it therapeutically. We need to conduct much more research. And even then it should only be given as a last resort, after weighing the benefits against the risk of harm."

Sessa is adamant that research into MDMA is justified. "Look at heroin. It's a class-A drug that's dangerous when used recreationally, but it's used widely in medicine, and so it should be—it's a very useful drug. Can you imagine saying to the Royal College of Anaesthetists, 'You can't use morphine or diamorphine [heroin] or pethidine or codeine or any opiate-based drugs because heroin is dangerous and people abuse it?' It's culturally bound. MDMA has been demonised."

In 2004, the most recent year for which there are records, 46 people died after taking Ecstasy, as against 8,221 alcohol-related deaths. And most of those who die with MDMA in their system have mixed it with substances such as alcohol or cannabis, which confounds the picture.

[In January 2008], the police chief for North Wales, Richard Brunstrom, called for the drug to be reclassified, claiming it was "safer than aspirin". He was widely shouted down, but Steve Rolles of Transform believes he may have a point. "It's not appropriate to have Ecstasy in class A. In terms of indicators of harm—toxicity, mortality, addictiveness and antisocial behaviour—it's not comparable to heroin or cocaine. But the government won't reclassify it. Reclassifying cannabis [from class B to C] in 2004 caused years of grief from opposition parties and the media."

The minister for drugs policy, Vernon Coaker, declined to comment on reclassification for medical purposes, but a spokesman said: "The government has no intention of reclassifying Ecstasy. It can and does kill unpredictably; there is no such thing as a 'safe dose'. We firmly believe it should remain a class-A drug. In addition, the government warns young people of the dangers of Ecstasy through the Frank campaign."

It does. But it also gives advice on safe Ecstasy use—or "harm minimisation". This is precisely the mixed message that Rolles believes is damaging. "Harm reduction is reducing the harm that's created by illegal supply in the first place," he says. "So you have harm-reduction, information within a legal framework that maximises harm. It's a clear contradiction."

The Problem of Funding

Then there is the problem of funding. MDMA therapy is based on the idea of a single treatment, or a course of treatment sessions, rather than long-term prescriptive use. This presents little or no benefit to drug companies that have huge budgets for research as long as there's a saleable product at the end. And if MDMA does prove effective, companies could stand to lose millions from lost sales of long-term antidepressants prescribed for PTSD.

Sessa says: "There's no financial incentive for the pharmaceutical companies to look into it. Psychotherapy is notoriously underfunded and discredited by the drug companies. It could benefit the government to look into MDMA, but their funding is a drop in the ocean next to a company like Pfizer's research budget. So who's going to pay for a multi-centre psychotherapy trial for 10,000 people—the couch-makers?"

PTSD therapy currently costs the NHS £14m a year, and with more veterans returning from Iraq and Afghanistan, that figure is set to rise. [In 2007], 1,200 new veterans sought treatment for PTSD from the organisation Combat Stress, compared with 300 in the year 2000. But realistically, would the government ever sanction MDMA research? "It's not impossible, but it's improbable," says Sessa. "It takes a very brave politician to look at the evidence and say, 'Well, there might be positive aspects to this class-A drug. Let's look into it. ' It's a conceptual, social battle which won't be easy to win."

10

The Illicit Drug Anti-Proliferation Act Deters Selling and Using Club Drugs

U.S. Drug Enforcement Administration (DEA)

The U.S. Drug Enforcement Administration (DEA), a part of the U.S. Department of Justice, enforces the controlled substances laws and regulations of the United States.

Enacted on April 30, 2003, the Illicit Drug Anti-Proliferation Act funds education programs on the dangers of club drugs and imposes harsher sentences for the use of GHB (gamma-hydroxybutyrate) in sexual assaults and crimes. Additionally, it penalizes promoters, property owners, or venue managers and employees who are involved in trafficking club drugs at raves and dance parties. Although they are alcohol-free events, raves are often a haven of club-drug distribution and use, from which rogue promoters profit. The act does not target legitimate raves, dancing to techno music, or events where drug dealing or use is incidental. Penalties only occur when prosecutors prove that a promoter or property owner willingly facilitated the distribution or use of club drugs.

The Illicit Drug Anti-Proliferation Act, enacted on April 30, 2003, is welcome news in the fight against Ecstasy, Predatory Drugs, and Methamphetamine. The Act protects kids from drugs in three distinct ways:

U.S. Drug Enforcement Administration (DEA), "New Drug Law Protects Children and FAQs About the Illicit Drug Anti-Proliferation Act," in USDOJ.Gov, 2003.

1. It authorizes funds to educate parents and kids on the dangers of Ecstasy and other predatory drugs;

2. It directs the United States Sentencing Commission to consider increasing federal sentencing penalties for offenses involving GHB, a predatory drug used to facilitate sexual assaults; and

3. It makes clear that anyone who knowingly opens, leases, rents, or maintains, whether permanently or temporarily, any place for the purpose of using, distributing or manufacturing any controlled substance, can be held accountable. The new law also makes it unlawful for a manager, employee or owner, to profit from, or make available for use, any place for the purpose of storing, distributing, manufacturing, or using a controlled substance.

Parents and teens often believe that events such as raves are safe and drug/alcohol-free. In reality, promoters often turn these events into havens of drug trafficking and use for their own illicit profit. This law is a helpful tool for law enforcement in addressing this problem.

The DEA [U.S. Drug Enforcement Administration] is committed to responsible enforcement of this law, which will shield innocent businesses from criminal liability for incidental drug use by patrons while eliminating unlawful enterprises that lure young people into dangerous drug use. Although the changes were necessary to close loopholes in existing law, the prosecution proof thresholds for "knowledge" and "intent" remain the same.

All DEA offices have been provided with updated guidance regarding the implementation of this new statute. This guidance also establishes procedures within DEA to obtain Headquarters review of proposed enforcement activity under the Act. This will ensure that all DEA activity under the Act complies with its terms and intent and with the First Amendment.

The Illicit Drug Anti-Proliferation Act

As a business owner, will I be arrested or fined because of illegal drug use by a patron?

No. Legitimate property owners and event promoters are not in violation of the law just because a patron engages in illegal drug activity on their property. DEA agents have clear guidance specifically advising them that property owners not personally involved in illicit drug activity are not in violation of the law.

I enjoy going to raves where I dance and listen to techno music. Is this law trying to close down rave clubs?

No. People may continue to attend and hold legitimate rave events. This law does not target dancing, music, or any other form of expression. Rather, it targets people who promote events for the purpose of distributing or using illicit drugs—regardless if there is any dancing or music at the event. The law applies only to people who knowingly and intentionally allow the distribution, manufacture, or use of illegal drugs at their event. Rave goers should be aware that illegal drugs are readily available at many raves and need to know two dangers. The first is that drugs like Ecstasy—that are often advertised and "tested" as safe, are neither. The tests are unreliable, and Ecstasy is never safe at any dosage level. The second is that GHB and other predatory drugs can be surreptitiously slipped into anyone's drink and used to commit sexual assault.

What if I host a private party and friends happen to light up a joint or pop an Ecstasy pill? Will the DEA use this law to arrest me?

No. This law only applies to people who control or manage a facility "for the purpose of unlawfully manufacturing, storing, distributing, or using a controlled substance." It does not apply to the activities of people in the privacy of their own homes. Nevertheless, it is important to remember that use and sale of illicit drugs anywhere remains illegal under the Controlled Substances Act.

What is the "crack house statute" I keep hearing about?

This law was enacted [in 1986] and became known as the "crack house statute" (21 USC 856). It permitted the Justice Department to prosecute property owners who knowingly and intentionally allowed others to use their property to hold events for the purpose of distributing or using drugs. For example, it was used to prosecute people such as motel owners and car repair shop owners who knowingly and intentionally allowed their premises to be used for drug distribution.

How does the new law change the "crack house statute?"

The newly enacted Illicit Drug Anti-Proliferation Act of 2003 amended the statute to make it more feasible to successfully prosecute rogue event promoters. It clarifies that the law applies to promoters as well as owners, to any location rather than just the previously defined "enclosures," and to one-night events as well as on-going events. The changes were necessary to close loopholes in existing law because rogue promoters could evade prosecution in several ways.

Won't it be easy for prosecutors to "prove" that an individual promoted an event for the purpose of drug use?

No. In fact, proving that an event is held for the purpose of drug use is a high legal threshold. It would not apply to events where people just happened to use drugs—a prosecutor would have to show that the promoter or property owner knew that a purpose of the event was the sale or use of drugs and the promoter or property owner took steps to facilitate and publicize that illicit activity and allowed it to occur.

How can citizens be sure that DEA agents across the country will enforce this law in a uniform manner?

All DEA offices have been provided with guidance regarding the implementation of this new statute. This guidance also establishes procedures within DEA to obtain Headquarters review of proposed enforcement activity under the Act. This will ensure that all DEA activity under the Act complies with its terms and intent and with the First Amendment.

11

The Illicit Drug Anti-Proliferation Act Is Unfair and Threatens Civil Liberties

Janelle Brown

A resident of Los Angeles, Janelle Brown is an author and journalist who frequently contributes to Vogue, *the* New York Times, *the* Los Angeles Times, *and* Wired. *She was a senior writer at Salon.com for five years.*

Previously submitted as the controversial, failed RAVE (Reducing American's Vulnerability to Ecstasy) Act, the Illicit Drug Anti-Proliferation Act was quietly piggybacked onto the AMBER Act (which set up a national kidnapping alert system) and passed on April 30, 2003. A loosely worded piece of legislation, the Illicit Drug Anti-Proliferation Act permits the indiscriminate shuttering of events and venues based on criteria that single out raves (techno music, glow sticks, chill-out rooms) and can be unjustly enforced to close hip-hop, gay, and other social functions authorities may deem undesirable. It also unfairly penalizes promoters and club owners who are not responsible for, do not profit from, or do not encourage drug use. Moreover, the act drives raves further underground, scaring promoters and club owners from participating in harm reduction and being prepared to ably respond to drug emergencies.

[O]n April 10, 2003] the House and Senate almost unanimously passed the National AMBER Alert Network Act of 2003, a popular bill that will soon create a nationwide kidnapping alert system. Coming in the wake of a year of high-profile child abductions—from Elizabeth Smart (whose parents supported the bill) to Samantha Runnion—the bill was a no-brainer, destined to pass quickly and smoothly through Congress.

Surely Joe Biden [Vice President and former Democratic senator from Delaware] knew this, which explains why he cannily sneaked his own, completely unrelated legislation into the AMBER Act just two days before the vote. Piggybacked onto the act was the Illicit Drug Anti-Proliferation Act, a thinly veiled rewrite of legislation that was controversial in 2002 and failed to make it to a vote on the Senate floor. Now, club owners and partyers alike are being subjected to a loosely worded and heavy-handed law that authorities will be able to indiscriminately use to shut down music events at any time they please, assuming they find evidence of drug use. Thanks to Biden's surreptitious efforts, a few glow sticks and a customer or two on Ecstasy could be all it takes to throw a party promoter in jail for 20 years.

The passing of the Illicit Drug Anti-Proliferation Act was sudden but not entirely out of the blue. Last year, the Illicit Drug Anti-Proliferation Act was known as the RAVE Act (the leadenly acronymed "Reducing Americans' Vulnerability to Ecstasy Act"), a piece of legislation designed by Biden in early 2002 to put rave promoters out of business. An expansion of the crack-house statute of 1986—which made crack-den proprietors liable for what took place in their homes, even if they didn't deal drugs themselves—the RAVE Act threatened those who "knowingly and intentionally rent, lease, profit from, or make available for use, with or without compensation, [a] place for the purpose of unlawfully manufacturing, storing, distributing, or using a controlled substance" with 20 years in jail and $250,000 in fines.

A New Weapon

In English, this meant that anyone who intentionally let people do drugs at their events could be held liable. It also expanded the crack-house statute in two significant ways: Now the law could be applied to one-night events—concerts, raves, parties, festivals—as well as permanent locales like nightclubs, and it added civil penalties for violations, lowering the burden of proof from "beyond reasonable doubt" to a "preponderance of evidence."

So what "preponderance of evidence" would authorities use to determine that the people who threw these parties "knowingly" let their customers and guests use drugs? The RAVE Act offered a handy list of "findings" that authorities could use as proof—including the presence of "overpriced bottles of water" and chill rooms, and the sale of glow sticks, massage oils and pacifiers (all of which are sometimes used to enhance the effects of Ecstasy). Never mind that all of the above can also be found at everything from 'N Sync concerts to an Earth Day festival; in the eyes of Biden and other like-minded officials and law enforcement officers (of which there are many), these are sinister drug paraphernalia that can only point to one thing.

Civil liberties groups and grass-roots activists from the electronic music community went on the defense. Infuriated ravers flooded Congress with letters, complaining that they were being singled out because of their lifestyle choices. The ACLU [American Civil Liberties Union] and the reform-minded Drug Policy Alliance convinced co-sponsoring Sens. Patrick Leahy, D-Vt., and Dick Durbin, D-Ill., that the vaguely written law could be used to limit freedom of expression and that businesses would unconstitutionally be held liable for their customers' actions. The two senators withdrew their support, and the RAVE Act finally died in committee last fall [2002].

But Biden was not deterred, and he reintroduced the bill in early 2003. This time, in order to nominally appease detractors, he changed the name of his bill to the less inflammatory "Illicit Drug Anti-Proliferation Act" and struck the "findings" section of the legislation. Then he swiftly tacked it on to the AMBER Act, where, without any kind of hearing and before the ACLU and grass-roots organizations could raise a stink, it finally passed.

The bill's opponents worry that the new law (which [was] signed by President [George W.] Bush. . .) will effectively quash the electronic music community. Most ravers don't object to the targeting of unprincipled rave promoters who do sell drugs to kids, but the law is so loosely worded that it could be used against anyone who throws parties that are unpopular with local authorities. After all, according to the new law, you don't actually need to be directly involved in providing drugs to customers to be found guilty; all you have to do is knowingly allow drug use to take place.

The police are no doubt delighted to have a new weapon to use in their skirmishes with clubs and late-night revelers (a feud that goes all the way back to the days of Prohibition). Do the local authorities have issues with your nightclub or party? All they would need to do is find a few drug users at your event and "prove" that you endorsed this activity by pointing at, say, your overpriced bottled water or the ambulances that you keep on standby in case of emergencies (a common practice at concerts and nightclubs alike), and they could shut you down, throw you in jail, and empty your bank account.

Say Goodbye to All-Night Dance Parties

Biden argues that this will never happen. "The purpose of my legislation is not to prosecute legitimate law-abiding managers of stadiums, arenas, performing arts centers, licensed beverage facilities and other venues because of incidental drug use at their events," he wrote when he introduced the Illicit Drug

Anti-Proliferation Act. "My bill would help in the prosecution of rogue promoters who not only know that there is drug use at their event but also hold the event for the purpose of illegal drug use or distribution."

The backward logic of this thinking punishes club owners and rave promoters for trying to keep their customers safe.

Unfortunately, precedents show otherwise. Biden's bill—even with the findings removed—formalizes what has been taking place in drug-enforcement circles for several years: Since 2000, authorities around the country have moved to shut down some of the nation's most popular dance parties, using the crack-house statue as a bludgeon and those glow sticks and chill rooms as their evidence. In many cities, such as San Diego and Fort Lauderdale, the police have even formed "Rave Task Forces"—and study DEA-provided fact sheets that detail drug paraphernalia (sports drinks! lollipops! eye drops!)—to shut down electronic music events and jail their promoters.

In New Orleans, for example, the promoters of one of the city's most popular dance clubs, Freebass, were charged with allowing drug use to take place at their events, despite an utter lack of evidence that they were in any way involved with or aware of drug sales. The promoters plea-bargained to avoid a costly lawsuit and ended up signing an injunction that forbade the presence of glow sticks, pacifiers, massage tables and chill rooms at any future parties (as if these were somehow to blame for the drug problem). And the Department of Alcohol and Beverage Control last week moved to shut down Ten 15 Folsom, one of the largest and most popular nightclubs in San Francisco, and accused the owners of permitting drug use to take place there. Once again, investigators pointed at the presence of glow sticks, as well as emergency medical technicians

[EMTs] (which, ironically, Ten 15 had begun providing, by court order, after several overdoses by customers) as evidence that the club owners endorsed drug use.

The backward logic of this thinking punishes club owners and rave promoters for trying to keep their customers safe. It is inevitable that some revelers at just about any kind of musical event—whether an Avril Lavigne concert or a techno dance club—are going to bring and consume drugs, no matter how diligently you search their pockets or how often you eject offenders. Club owners and party promoters are aware of this (who isn't?) and often do everything they can to both limit this activity and prevent tragedies among those who pop pills anyway. It's quite possible that the Illicit Drug Anti-Proliferation Act will force panicky promoters to reconsider providing ambulances or EMTs, lest those be used as "evidence" against them. Already, many parties have stopped harm-reduction groups like DanceSafe from coming to their events to pass out safety literature or anonymously test Ecstasy pills to ensure that they aren't more lethal concoctions.

Once the president signs the bill, promoters may consider the risks and never throw parties at all. Others will simply move their parties underground to illegal locations (abandoned warehouses, empty buildings, remote fields) where they are less likely to be found by authorities but more likely to be providing an unsafe setting for their customers.

The Enemy Du Jour

The law isn't limited to electronic music events, either. Civil liberties experts worry that it could be used as a tool of bigotry to shut down hip-hop or gay-circuit parties. In a worst-case scenario, the DEA could even bust you for a private barbecue in your home where friends light up a bong: After all, the new law covers private residences, too. That may be unlikely, but the DEA is no stranger to badly conceived drug raids.

No one is arguing that drug use doesn't take place at raves and nightclubs and concerts, that kids don't sometimes use glow sticks or pacifiers to enhance their high, or that drugs aren't harmful—occasionally lethal—for kids. But in its rush to stamp out America's current drug demon, Ecstasy, this sweeping and illogical legislation instead violates basic civil liberties and labels entire communities as the enemy.

All these concerns may very well have come out during public debate on the law—but, of course, that never happened. Immediately after the AMBER Alert was passed, Sen. Leahy issued a press release complaining about the unrelated legislation that was piggybacked on the bill, singling out the Illicit Drug Anti-Proliferation Act as one of the worst offenders. "Business owners have come to Congress and told us there are only so many steps they can take to prevent any of the thousands of people who may attend a concert or a rave from using drugs, and they are worried about being held personally accountable for the illegal acts of others," he wrote. "Those concerns may well be overstated, but they deserve a fuller hearing. . . . I think we would have been well-served by making a greater effort to find out."

Too late. Instead, yet another badly conceived piece of drug legislation, capriciously taking aim at the enemy du jour, was rammed through the system before more rational voices could discuss it. The vote took a matter of minutes and no thought whatsoever; the repercussions of the law will be felt for years.

Organizations to Contact

The editors have compiled the following list of organizations concerned with the issues debated in this book. The descriptions are derived from materials provided by the organizations. All have publications or information available for interested readers. The list was compiled on the date of publication of the present volume; names, addresses, phone and fax numbers, and e-mail and Internet addresses may change. By aware that many organizations take several weeks or longer to respond to inquiries, so allow as much time as possible.

American Council for Drug Education (ACDE)
164 West 74th Street, New York, NY   10023
(800) 488-3784
e-mail: acde@phoenixhouse.org
Web site: www.acde.org

The American Council for Drug Education informs the public about the harmful effects of abusing drugs and alcohol. It was created by Phoenix House, the largest private substance abuse treatment program in the United States. Among its publications are the Drug Awareness Series of brochures that provide information on illegal drugs.

Canadian Centre on Substance Abuse (CCSA)
75 Albert Street, Suite 300, Ottawa, ON   K1P 5E7
  Canada
(613) 235-4048 • fax: (613) 235-8101
e-mail: info@ccsa.ca
Web site: www.ccsa.ca

The CCSA works to minimize the harm associated with the use of alcohol, tobacco, and other drugs by sponsoring public debates on this issue. It disseminates information on the nature, extent, and consequences of substance abuse and supports organizations involved in substance abuse treatment, prevention, and educational programming. The center publishes the newsletter *Action News*.

Canadian Foundation for Drug Policy (CFDP)

70 MacDonald Street, Ottawa, ON K2P 1116
    Canada
(613) 236-1027 • fax: (613) 238-2891
e-mail: eoscapel@cfdp.ca
Web site: www.cfdp.ca

Founded by several of Canada's leading drug policy specialists, the CFDP examines the objectives and consequences of Canada's drug laws and polities. When necessary, the foundation recommends alternatives that it believes would make Canada's drug policies more effective and humane. The CFDP discusses drug policy issues with the Canadian government, media, and general public. It also disseminates educational materials and maintains a Web site.

Cato Institute

1000 Massachusetts Avenue, NW
Washington, DC   20001-5403
(202) 842-0200 • fax: (202) 842-3490
Web site: www.cato.org

The institute is a public-policy research foundation dedicated to limiting the control of government and to protecting individual liberty. Cato, which strongly favors drug legalization, publishes the *Cato Journal* three times a year and the *Cato Policy Report* bimonthly.

Center for Cognitive Liberty and Ethics (CCLE)

P.O. Box 73481, Davis, CA   95617-3481
fax: (530) 570-7912
e-mail: info@cognitiveliberty.org
Web site: www.cognitiveliberty.org

The Center for Cognitive Liberty and Ethics is a nonprofit organization dedicated to protecting and advancing freedom of thought in the area of neurotechnologies. CCLE works to ensure that the application and regulation of new psychotropic drugs and neurotechnologies proceed with as few restrictions as possible and is consistent with the fundamental right to freedom of thought. CCLE publishes *Mind Matter*, a quarterly newsletter; the *Journal of Cognitive Liberty*, a quarterly journal; various flyers and pamphlets; and maintains a Web site.

Center on Addiction and Substance Abuse (CASA)
633 3rd Avenue, 19th Floor, New York, NY   10017-6706
(212) 841-5200
Web site: www.casacolumbia.org

CASA is a private, nonprofit organization that works to educate the public about the hazards of chemical dependency. The organization supports treatment as the best way to reduce chemical dependency. It produces publications describing the harmful effects of alcohol and drug addiction and effective ways to address the problem of substance abuse. It also distributes the monthly newsletter *START* and maintains a Web site.

DanceSafe
8100-M4 Wyoming Boulevard, NE, #116
Albuquerque, NM   87713
e-mail: dsusa@dancesafe.org
Web site: www.dancesafe.org

DanceSafe is a nonprofit harm-reduction organization promoting health and safety within the rave and club communities. It provides information on drugs, safe sex, and other health issues and offers pill testing and adulterant screening. DanceSafe maintains a Web site and an online bookstore.

Drug Enforcement Administration (DEA)
Mailstop AES, Springfield, VA   22152
(202) 307-1000
Web site: www.dea.gov

The DEA is the federal agency charged with enforcing the nation's drug laws. The agency concentrates on stopping the smuggling and distribution of narcotics in the United States and abroad. It publishes the annual *Drugs of Abuse* manual.

Drug Policy Alliance

70 West 36th Street, 16th Floor, New York, NY 10018
(212) 613-8020 • fax: (212) 613-8021
e-mail: nyc@drugpolicy.org
Web site: www.drugpolicy.org

The Drug Policy Alliance is working to broaden the public debate on drug policy and to promote alternatives to the war on drugs based on science, compassion, health and human rights. The organization promotes harm reduction, an alternative approach to drug policy and treatment that focuses on minimizing the adverse effects of both drug use and drug prohibition. The alliance's published research briefs, fact sheets, and articles are available on its Web site.

Institute for Social Research at the University of Michigan

426 Thompson Street, Ann Arbor, MI 48104-2321
(734) 764-8354 • fax: (734) 647-4575
e-mail: isr-info@isr.umich.edu
Web site: www.isr.umich.edu

The institute conducts the annual Monitoring the Future Survey, which gathers data on drug use—including club drug use—and attitudes toward drugs among eighth-, tenth-, and twelfth-grade students. Survey results are published by the National Institute on Drug Abuse.

Libertarian Party

2600 Virginia Avenue, NW, Suite 200, Washington, DC 20037
(800) 353-2887
e-mail: info@lp.org
Web site: www.lp.org

The Libertarian Party is a political party whose goal is to protect individual rights and liberties. It advocates the repeal of all laws prohibiting the production, sale, possession, or use of drugs. The party believes law enforcement should focus on preventing violent crimes against persons and property rather than on prosecuting people who use drugs. It publishes the bimonthly *Libertarian Party News* and periodic *Issues Papers* and distributes a compilation of articles supporting drug legalization.

Multidisciplinary Association for Psychedelic Studies (MAPS)

10424 Love Creek Road, Ben Lomond, CA   95005
(831) 336-4325 • fax: (831) 336-3665
e-mail: askmaps@maps.org
Web site: www.maps.org

The Multidisciplinary Association for Psychedelic Studies is a research and educational organization that assists scientists to design, fund, obtain approval for, and report on studies into the risks and benefits of MDMA (Ecstasy), psychedelic drugs, and marijuana. MAPS maintains a Web site and an online bookstore.

National Institute on Drug Abuse (NIDA)

6001 Executive Boulevard, Room 5213
Bethesda, MD   20892-9561
(301) 443-1124
e-mail: information@nida.nih.gov
Web site: www.nida.nih.gov

NIDA supports and conducts research on drug abuse—including the yearly Monitoring the Future Survey—in order to improve addiction prevention, treatment, and policy efforts. It publishes the bimonthly *NIDA Notes* newsletter, the periodic *NIDA Capsules* fact sheets, and a catalog of research reports and public education materials such as *Marijuana: Facts for Teens.*

Office of National Drug Control Policy (ONDCP)

Executive Office of the President
Drugs and Crime Clearinghouse
Rockville, MD   20849-6000

(800) 666-3332 • fax: (301) 519-5212
Web site: www.whitehousedrugpolicy.gov

The Office of National Drug Control Policy is responsible for formulating the government's national drug strategy and the president's antidrug policy as well as coordinating the federal agencies responsible for stopping drug trafficking. Drug policy studies are available upon request.

RAND Corporation
1700 Main Street, Santa Monica, CA   90407-2138
(310) 393-0411
Web site: www.rand.org

The RAND Corporation is a research institution that seeks to improve public policy through research and analysis. RAND's Drug Policy Research Center publishes information on the costs, prevention, and treatment of alcohol and drug abuse as well as on trends in drug-law enforcement.

Reason Foundation
3451 South Sepulveda Boulevard, Suite 400
Los Angeles, CA   90034
(310) 391-2245
Web site: www.reason.org

This public-policy organization researches contemporary social and political problems and promotes libertarian philosophy and free-market principles. It publishes the monthly *Reason* magazine, which contains articles and editorials critical of the war on drugs and smoking regulation.

Bibliography

Books

Stan Beeler	*Dance, Drugs, and Escape: The Club Scene in Literature, Film, and Television Since the Late 1980s.* Jefferson, NC: McFarland, 2007.
John Hoffman and Susan Froemke	*Addiction: Why Can't They Just Stop?* Emmaus, PA: Rodale, 2007.
Tara Koellhoffer	*Ecstasy and Other Club Drugs.* New York: Chelsea House, 2008.
Cynthia Kuhn, Scott Swartzwelder, Wilkie Wilson, and Leigh Heather Wilson	*Buzzed: The Straight Facts About the Most Used and Abused Drugs from Alcohol to Ecstasy (3rd ed.).* New York: Norton, 2008.
Tim Pilcher	*E: The Incredibly Strange History of Ecstasy.* Philadelphia, PA: Running Press, 2008.
Trinka Porrata	*G'd Up 24/7: The GHB Addiction Guide.* San Clemente, CA: Lawtech, 2007.
Bill Sanders	*Drugs, Clubs, and Young People: Sociological and Public Health Perspectives.* Burlington, VT: Ashgate, 2006.

Katherine Swarts, ed.   *The History of Drugs: Club Drugs.* Farmington Hills, MI: Greenhaven Press, 2005.

Periodicals

David Adam   "Treating Agony with Ecstasy," *Guardian*, February 17, 2005.

Keith Bradsher   "Coating on Toy Beads from China Could Be Life-Threatening," *International Herald Tribune*, November 7, 2007.

Jonathan Darman   "Out of the Club, Onto the Couch," *Newsweek*, December 5, 2003.

Meghan Daum   "Long, Strange Trip to Ecstasy," *Los Angeles Times*, May 3, 2008.

Amin Ghaziani   "The Circuit Party's Faustian Bargain," *Gay & Lesbian Review*, July–August 2005.

Richard Maffeo   "Drug's Deadly Kid-Friendly Face: Is That Really a Sweet Tart?" *Vibrant Life*, November–December 2006.

Mike Males   "This Is Your Brain on Drugs, Dad," *New York Times*, January 3, 2007.

Caspar Melville   "Writhing on Ecstasy," *New Humanist*, July–August 2004.

Thijs Niemantsverdriet   "Goodbye, Fungus Fix," *Newsweek*, October 22, 2007.

Simon Reynolds   "The Turn Away from the Turntable,"
New York Times, January 23, 2005.

ScienceDaily   "LSD Treatment for Alcoholism Gets
New Look," October 9, 2006.

Carla Spartos   "Party Patrol," *Village Voice*, April 22,
2003.

Maia Szalavitz   "Tackling Depression with Ketamine,"
New Scientist, January 20, 2007.

Zak Szymanski   "Dangerous Mix: Date-Rape Drugs:
Not Just a Straight Thing Anymore,"
Curve, November 2003.

Stephen Watson   "The Agony of Ecstasy," *Buffalo News*,
and Dan Herbeck   December 19, 2004.

Index

A

Abuse
  in clubs, 23, 26, 32
  prevention, 40
  research, 42
  scope of, 44–46
  sexual, 27, 39
  by teens/young adults, 31
  vs. use, 28
ACLU (American Civil Liberties Union), 83–84
Addiction, 37, 42, 50–51, 69
Advisory Council on Misuse of Drugs, 7
Alcoholics Anonymous (AA), 40
AMBER Alert Network Act of 2003, 81–82, 84, 87
American Civil Liberties Union (ACLU), 83–84
Antidepressants, 24–27, 63, 74
Archives of General Psychiatry (journal), 52

B

Benzodiazepine, 15–16
Berezansky, Paula, 21
Betts, Leah, 63, 65
Biden, Joe, 82, 84–85
Brain damage/activity, 28–29, 48–50
Bristol University, 7, 71
Brunstrom, Richard, 7, 73
Bush, George W., 84

C

Center for AIDS Prevention Studies (CAPS), 36
Centers for Disease Control and Prevention, 28

Civil liberties, 83, 87
  See also Illicit Drug Anti-Proliferation Act; ACLU
Clark, Judith, 19, 22
Classification
  GHB, 14–15, 19, 73–74
  MDMA, 8–9, 12
Clinician Administered PTSD Scale (CAPS), 69
Clinton, Bill, 19
Club drugs
  awareness, lack of, 30
  effects, 11
  HIV risk, 36, 38–39, 46
  popularity, 11
  treatment options, 39–40
  use, 12, 37–38, 39
  vs. other drugs, 11
  See also GHB (gamma-hydroxybutyrate); Illicit Drug Anti-Proliferation Act; Ketalar; MDMA (methylenedioxymethamphetamine); Rohypnol
Coaker, Vernon, 74
Columbia University National Survey of American Attitudes on Substance Abuse, 12
Community Epidemiology Working Group, 12
Crack house statue, 79, 82
Crystal Meth Anonymous (CMA), 40

D

Dance parties, 84–86
DanceSafe, 40, 86
Date rape
  prohibition act, 19
  prosecution barriers, 21

Date rape drug, 14, 16, 18–19
    See also Rohypnol
Davis, David, 9
Depression, long-term, 58–60
Depression treatment, 24–27
    See also Posttraumatic stress
    disorder (PTSD)
Doblin, Rick, 26–27, 70–71
Dopamine, 48, 60
Drug abuse
    in clubs, 23, 26, 32
    prevention, 40
    research, 42
    by teens/young adults, 31
    vs. use, 28
Drug Abuse Warning Network, 20,
    45
Drug Enforcement Administration
    (DEA), 11, 20, 44, 71, 77
Drug Policy Alliance, 83
Drugs policy, 9
Durbin, Dick, 83
Dworkin, Ronald, 25

E

Ecstasy
    classification, 8
    as gateway drug, 58, 61
    as harmful, 8–9
    and memory function, 9
    price of, 61
    as safe, 7, 9
    vs. other drugs, 7
    See also MDMA
    (methylenedioxymetham-
    phetamine)
Electronic music community, 83,
    84
Emory University, 24
Entactogens, 10–11

F

Farias, Hillory, 19
Flashbacks
    Ketamine, 17, 34
    MDMA, 63
    PTSD, 66
Flunitrazepam. *See* Rohypnol
Food and Drug Administration
    (FDA), 44, 52

G

Gamma-hydroxybutyrate (GHB).
    See GHB (gamma-
    hydroxybutyrate)
Gatehouse, Jimmy, 58–61
Gateway drug, 58, 61
GHB (gamma-hydroxybutyrate)
    availability, 19–21
    dangers/risks, 33
    as date rape drug, 18
    overview discussion, 14–15
    prosecution barriers, 21–22

H

Hanson, Glen, 59–60
Harvey, Cassandra, 18–19, 20
Harvey, Joshua, 18–19, 20
Hillory J. Farias and Samantha
    Reid Date Rape Drug Prohibi-
    tion Act of 2000, 19
HIV risk, 36, 38–39, 46
Holland, Julie, 8
Hudson Institute, 25

I

Illicit Drug Anti-Proliferation Act
    business/property owners, 78
    civil liberties, 83, 87
    crack house statue, 79
    DEA responsibility, 77

evidence, 83
implementation, 80
incidental drug use, 84
legal threshold, 79
private parties, 78–79, 86
protections, 76–77
rave clubs, 78
INSIGHT, 24–26
Internet, drug availability, 19–21

J

Jaehne, Emily, 8
Johns Hopkins University, 28, 71

K

Ketalar. *See* Ketamine
Ketamine, 16–17, 34–35
Kilgore, Donna, 62–63, 65–68

L

Laws. *See* Hillory J. Farias and
    Samantha Reid Date Rape Drug
    Prohibition Act of 2000; Illicit
    Drug Anti-Proliferation Act
Leahy, Patrick, 83, 87
Love drug. *See* MDMA
    (methylenedioxymetham-
    phetamine)

M

MAPS (Multidisciplinary Associa-
    tion for Psychedelic Studies), 26,
    52, 70–71
MDMA (methylenedioxymetham-
    phetamine)
    abuse/abusers, 44–46
    addiction, 50
    brain damage/activity, 28–29,
        48–50
    changing hearts/minds, 71–74
    classification, 74

controls, 27–28
criminalization, 64–65
dangers/risks, 32–33
deaths, 26–27, 73
depression treatment use, 23,
    25–26
development, 12
effects, 13–14, 24, 42–43, 46–
    48, 73
funding problem, 74–75
history, 44
media misrepresentations,
    52–57
monitored use, 69–71
prevention programs, 50–51
therapeutic use, 8, 23, 44, 64
treatment options, 51
See also ecstasy
Media misrepresentations, 52–57
Merck (pharmaceutical company),
    64
Methamphetamine, 33–34, 38
Methylenedioxymethamphetamine
    (MDMA). *See* MDMA
    (methylenedioxymethamphet-
    amine)
Mithoefer, Annie, 68–71
Mithoefer, Michael, 63, 64, 68–71
Monitoring the Future (MTF)
    survey, 45
Mulligan, James, 60–61
Multidisciplinary Association for
    Psychedelic Studies (MAPS), 26,
    52, 70–71
Music community, 83, 84

N

Narcotics Anonymous (NA), 40
National Drug Intelligence Center,
    21
National Institute on Drug Abuse
    (NIDA), 42, 45–46

Netherlands XTC Toxicity (NeXT), 52

New York University, 8

North Wales Police, 7, 9, 73

Nutt, David, 7, 9

O

Oberlin, Max, 64

O'Callaghan, James, 28

O'Meara, Kelly Patricia, 25

Operation Webslinger, 20–21

Oster, Bessie, 31

P

Partnership for a Drug-Free America, 12

Paxil, 24

PCP (phencyclidine), 16

Pfizer (pharmaceutical company), 74–75

Phoenix House, 31, 61

Police
    Illicit Drug Anti-Proliferation Act, 84
    training, 21, 40

Porrata, Trinka, 21–22

Posttraumatic stress disorder (PTSD)
    MDMA as treatment, 62–63, 69, 72
    therapy costs, 74–75

Prosecution
    barriers to, 21–22
    crack house statue, 79
    Illicit Drug Anti-Proliferation Act, 84–85
    proof thresholds, 77, 79

PROTECT project, 40

Prozac, 24–25

Psychotherapy
    for PTSD, 63–64, 69
    underfunding, 74–75

Psychotropics, 23–25, 27–29

R

RAVE (Reducing American's Vulnerability to Ecstasy) Act, 81–83

Raves, 30–32, 36–40, 76–78, 81–87

Reid, Samantha, 18–19, 22

Ricaurte, George, 28, 71

Rohypnol, 15–16, 34

Rolles, Steve, 65, 73–74

Roofies. *See* Rohypnol

Runnion, Samantha, 82

S

Schilt, Thelma, 9

Schoor, Albert von, 64

Seabrook House, 60–61

Serotonin production, 60

Serotonin selective reuptake inhibitors (SSRIs), 24–27, 56–57

Serotonin syndrome, 13

Sessa, Ben, 71–72, 74–75

Sexual abuse, 27, 39

Shulgin, Alexander, 64

Smart, Elizabeth, 82

Spinks, Lorna, 65

Stepping Stone (drug treatment center), 40

Stone, Caleb, 19–20

Strong, Ronald, 20

Substance Abuse and Mental Health Services Administration, 45

T

Transform (drug-policy reform group), 65, 73–74

Trevino, Ariel, 30–32

Twelve Step programs, 40

U

University of Adelaide, 8
University of Amsterdam, 9, 73
University of Michigan Monitoring the Future Study, 11–12
University of Utah, 59
U.S. Drug Enforcement Administration (DEA), 11, 20, 44, 71, 77
U.S. Food and Drug Administration (FDA), 44, 52
U.S. National Drug Intelligence Center, 20

V

Valium, 72
Verbal memory, 53–56
Viagra, 41

W

Win, Maartje de, 73

Z

Zoloft, 24